SPEAK IN PUBLIC
WITH CONFIDENCE

Maggie Eyre's website: www.maggieeyre.com

SPEAK
IN PUBLIC
WITH
CONFIDENCE

Maggie Eyre

RIGHT WAY

Constable & Robinson Ltd
3 The Lanchesters
162 Fulham Palace Road
London W6 9ER
www.right-way.co.uk
www.constablerobinson.com

A copy of the British Library Cataloguing in Publication Data
is available from the British Library

ISBN: 978-0-7160-2198-8
Printed and bound in the EU

1 3 5 7 9 10 8 6 4 2

DEDICATION

I dedicate this book to my friend and colleague Will Wesson who shared his clients with me and opened doors in the UK. I will honour his memory always through good work, good communication and 'just being Maggie'.

CONTENTS

ACKNOWLEDGEMENTS

I would like to thank:

Tom Bradley, for sowing the seed at the beginning in 2001. Thank you for introducing me to my first publisher Ian Watt who guided me all the way as a budding author.

Benny Thomas and Gareth St John Thomas at Exisle Publishing, thank you for making it possible for my book to sell in Australia, the UK and India. You are an author's dream come true. Your friendship and ongoing belief in me has made the sacrifices worth every word. You have set me on a new path as an author. I will forever be grateful. You took my knowledge to market with a quality team. Thanks to you my book has a long shelf life.

Judith Mitchell, my Editor at Constable Robinson, for your continued commitment and support.

Maggie Warbrick, my friend and business partner, who persisted with your vision of my work which knows no boundaries. Thank you for being my life line and confidante between Stockholm and London. Our vision of a Maggie-Maggie duo is the best new act for our clients in the UK,

Europe and the Middle East. I have recreated myself with your support and love.

Marilyn Waring, my friend of 30 years. You taught me to take risks and set my public speaking career in motion. You stand by me in the dark and in the light. Thank you for sharing your speaking adventures in Europe with me. You shake up audiences in many cultures and I still learn from you.

Penelope Sellers-Barr, whose unconditional friendship has enabled me to live in London. Thank you for your ongoing professional advice and your contribution to this book. I would not be in the UK without your support.

Vivien Bridgwater, for giving me love and wisdom. I am inspired to know you. Thank you for challenging me all the way and expanding my thinking. You have given me a purpose in this life.

Stuart Nash, who is dedicated to my progress in the UK. Thank you for believing in me. Fresh Eyre will grow with your business hat on.

Mark Scott for helping me to make sound professional decisions in Britain. Your fight with cancer gave me a reason to live every day with hope. Your friendship has been a highlight over the years. Thank you for battling for your life.

Giulia Sirignani, my inspirational girlfriend, for being another pair of eyes and point of view during the second re-write. The serendipity that brought us together has given me comfort, stimulation and a peace that comes from knowing that when all is sadness we share each other's joy. Thank you for your love and outstanding friendship and Lake Bracciano, Italy, my sanctuary where I can be creative and always be myself with your family, Gus and Matilda. You are a role model of an unstoppable woman.

Liz Greenslade, I thank you for your nurturing friendship, unflagging interest in the book and for the support on email and phone around the world.

John Sinclair. Thank you, John, for being a mentor and friend. Your faith in me enabled me to leave the safety net of my homeland to embark on a new adventure in the UK. Without you, this would not have been possible.

Mary Fenick, for introducing me to your beloved Will and continuing to support me as an author despite your massive loss. Your generous gift to me was to create opportunities.

Lorae Parry, you have been my rock here in London. Thank you for making me laugh when I wanted to give up.

Cliff Kimber and Pete Lawrence at Big Blue stuff for taking me under your brotherly wings and giving me endless moral support and advice.

Alexsei Belov, my new friend, for your many photo shoots for my work in the UK. Thank you for the book photo.

Gleb Pavlov, thank you for your friendship and respect. Your commitment as my hairdresser in long photo shoots was appreciated.

Sophie Mexted, my god daughter. Your efficiency, generosity and organizational skills made a gigantic difference.

My mother, Jean Eyre, for teaching me that communication is about being honest and authentic. You are the funniest, kindest and most generous woman I know. You left school at thirteen to help raise seven brothers and sisters. The greatest gift you have given me is my education and my freedom. You are my big love.

The four men in my life: my brothers Eddie, Tony, Michael and Robert, for being my biggest fans and loving me from ten thousand miles away. You enable me to have my freedom while caring for our mother. I have always been in your hearts. I have never left you. Thank you for your support and passion for my writing and career.

Acknowledgements

My dear clients, I appreciate you for attending my workshops and coaching sessions. To all the companies in the UK who have allowed me to step into your boardrooms to work with your most valuable asset, your people. Your investment is their personal growth.

I am indebted to all of my teachers over the years for their encouragement and showing me how to be embrace humanity. You all have been profoundly inspirational in my personal and professional life, opening the global doors to my dreams. Roger McGill for giving my life direction and purpose. His dramatic exit in 2008 after being hit by forked lightning, nature's way of reminding me of the influence he was, and still is, in my teaching. Roger was one of the most talented business presentation skills teachers in the world.

To the Maynard Leigh team, thank you for providing my clients with the perfect creative theatre business environment at your elegant studios in Central London.

And to you, the reader, thank you for giving me a reason to write and the opportunity to share my work with you on the international stage. I wrote this book for you, in order to make a difference in the world, to help you to live more powerfully, with greater courage, with a finer spirit of hope and joy when you speak. May you create a Presence wherever you are. I stand silently at your side, on your stage, to applaud your courage to speak out like you have never spoken before. Without you, there is no book; with you, there is possibility to grow and learn. You give me this gift and I am grateful forever.

PREFACE

Having the confidence and skills to deliver clear and concise public messages is a requirement for success in politics and in many other kinds of jobs.

Those of us who have made hundreds and even thousands of speeches over the years believe our significant experience has taught us how to deliver speeches effectively. But that is not always the case. Thus many seek advice on effective public speaking from those like Maggie Eyre who specialize in presentation skills.

I consulted Maggie after I became Leader of the Opposition. She helped me improve my overall presentation to my long-term benefit.

As Prime Minister I make hundreds of speeches a year at home and abroad. The advice I received from Maggie all those years ago still stands. I hope others will benefit from taking the advice which Maggie Eyre conveys here.

Helen Clark
Prime Minister of New Zealand
Minister for Arts, Culture and Heritage

INTRODUCTION

It is never too late to be what we might have been.
George Eliot

Sometimes life hands you opportunities – you have a choice to fly with them and blossom, or stand still and stagnate. The day I heard that a UK publisher wanted my book, I felt exhilarated as well as rewarded and vindicated in having moved my life and work to London.

Revising this book has given me an opportunity to reflect on how my new clients in the UK, Europe and the Middle East have convinced me that all the peoples of the world have one thing in common – they know how to communicate. So why not make it effective? And why not do whatever it takes to get it right?

I've had to be more self-disciplined and walk my own talk than at any other time in my life, persevering when a part of me was aching to give up. In listening to my publishers' requests to keep writing, and their belief in my work, the book is now published in Australia, New Zealand, India and the UK. And this last edition is by far the one of which I'm most

proud because it is the sum of my growth as a writer and
teacher in the art of communication.

The biggest joy and satisfaction have been revising the
book for the UK and finishing the manuscript for this third
edition on the shores of Lake Bracciano under an Italian sun.
I am a people person, and writing is lonely, but I have had
enormous support from a growing range of people all over the
world who have believed in me. Without them, this book
would not be on the shelf.

You can overcome your fear or phobia of public speaking
just as I overcame my nervousness about revising this book. I
believe you can overcome anything with will and determination. Speaking easily requires practice and a willingness to
connect with human beings. Never give up on your desire to
be extraordinary in everything you do, especially in your
communication. As one of the twentieth century's master
communicators declared:

> Some men see things as they are and say why?
> I dream things that never were and say why not.
>
> *Robert Kennedy*

What's important is that you stretch yourself further, have
higher expectations and have some fun doing it. When the first
edition of this book was still just an idea, I never imagined I
would actually enjoy writing and how in doing it my world
would open up in the way that it has. I remember when writing
ceased to be a chore, when I stopped talking about it as if it
was an impossible mountain I had to climb. My thoughts
changed – I started to practise what I preached with my
clients. I began to write with ease and enjoyment when I
decided not to judge the outcome. You may be a beginner,
writing or making your first speech; you may be an experienced, confident public speaker. It doesn't matter.

Be passionate about everything you take on, no matter how impossible or small it seems. Approach it with absolute commitment and zeal. Worry less about how you'll come across, and start to speak from your heart in a way that perhaps you never have before. Take off the armour, peel away the layers and step into the spotlight. Use your real stories to liven up your speech. Tell the audience your secrets, your thoughts, your dreams – share details you've never shared before about your mistakes, successes and hopes. Worry less about what people think of you.

You are special; your stories are unique and no one can tell your stories like you can. Courage is all you need! Speak from your heart and your listeners will be proud of your bravery. Stories help to turn an otherwise dull business presentation into something memorable.

Since embarking on this book I've talked to so many people who tell me their number-one secret is their fear of speaking in public. Move past the fear. Don't make it bigger than it is. Start today, and take small steps to master this craft that can change your life for the better. Live, work, speak to your full potential.

Please pass this book on to someone who needs it or use it when you lose your confidence. Lend it to friends or work colleagues. Don't let it be another personal-development text that attracts the cobwebs on your bookshelf. Let it remind you, you're the perfect person to give the speech you're about to deliver.

Create a new life for yourself, a world without fear. A world where you speak up, you speak out, you express yourself with truth. Dedicate your life to moving people. And make them want to listen to you.

Maggie Eyre

1

DEVELOPING CONFIDENCE

If all my talents were to be taken from me by some inscrutable providence, and I had my choice of keeping but one, I would unhesitatingly ask to be allowed to keep the power of speaking, for through it I would quickly recover all the rest.

Daniel Webster, Presentations Plus

You *can* overcome your fear of speaking in public.

Read this book, scribble all over it and make it yours. It contains the knowledge you need to become a better public speaker and a confident communicator. Throughout, I'll tell you my story, and the stories of many others who have conquered their fear of speaking in public. Learn from them, and embark on a journey to become more self-assured.

This book is for anyone, not just for a business audience. Perhaps you won't need to give a formal speech behind a microphone, but you can still use your public-speaking skills during informal talks or in meetings. Although I work with business people in the UK and around the world, helping them to improve their public-speaking skills, this book is relevant to anyone who wants to improve the way they communicate.

Whether it be a sales presentation, a job interview or a speech at a wedding, at some stage in our lives we all need to speak in public.

I believe that we teach what we need to learn. I teach public-speaking confidence programmes and yet this used to be my number one fear. Every time I stand up in front of a large audience now, I'm reminded of how much confidence is needed to perform. I've seen some of my clients go from having no confidence whatsoever to finding the courage to perform – and to enjoy themselves while doing so. You just need to be willing to step outside your comfort zone. No more excuses! It's not always easy, but I've come a long way – and so will you.

What is confidence?

The dictionary defines confidence as 'firm trust, a feeling of reliance or certainty, a sense of self-reliance, and boldness'. The key word for me is 'trust' – to develop confidence we need to trust ourselves and trust the audience we are speaking to. Your self-esteem will increase when you take risks and be bold. We need to rely on the wealth of experience that we have within. Trust in your message – you are worth listening to. Self-belief is everything as without it, we feel empty and lack self-assurance.

> Confidence doesn't come out of nowhere. It's a result of something . . . hours and days and weeks and years of constant work and dedication.
> *Roger Staubach*

Eleanor Roosevelt said, 'No one can make you feel inferior without your consent.' I often refer to these words and work daily on improving my self-confidence.

Fear

Fear is a natural reaction to public speaking – you're not going mad, you're not inadequate, and you're not incompetent. You are wonderfully human and all you need is a confidence tool kit and lots of practice to build your self-esteem. Did you know some people are more afraid of public speaking than dying? In the theatre we used to say 'we're dying out there' when we suffered from stage fright. I still relive that feeling in my dreams over and over. The good news is you can look natural even when you're terrified inside.

Fear is the mind killer, the little death.
Frank Herbert Dune

It constantly surprises me that so many of us are frightened of speaking in public. We spend so much of our lives communicating, so why don't we make more of an investment in getting it right? We need to communicate our ideas clearly and with ease.

All the great speakers were bad speakers first.
Ralph Emerson

Great speakers weren't born that way; they learn a craft and eventually it comes naturally. François Mitterand failed his orals at university because of stage fright. Winston Churchill didn't start out as a skilled writer or speaker either – he also failed at school. By his early twenties, his mother despaired of his ever becoming a success. Churchill topped his political career with a Nobel Prize for literature. When I want to give up on my dreams and lose confidence, I think of this memorable orator.

Even Steven Spielberg feared public speaking. Every skilled speaker you observe, know or admire didn't start out as an expert – they've had to learn how to speak in public, the same as you.

What are we afraid of?

Over the years my clients give the same reason for their dislike of public speaking: they are afraid of making a fool of themselves and not being taken seriously. It's natural to want the audience to believe in us and to want to appear credible. People are afraid of losing their way and feeling as though they are out of control. They dread getting stuck during a speech and not finding the right words. They fear negative feedback. Does any of this sound like you? I certainly used to feel this way.

Everything is a story. The mind spins stories out and you believe what the mind tells you. Every time you are stressed out or fearful you are believing what the mind is telling you.
Katie Byron

When clients start working with me, I talk to them about their schooling years and ask questions about the first moment they dreaded public speaking. There is often a specific event or time when they felt embarrassed in public. This incident, which often seems insignificant, remains fresh in their minds. The important thing is to accept that the past is the past, and today is a fresh start.

What inspires us?

I want to share with you a story about a formidable communicator who touched and inspired me.

Alain Roth lives in Paris and travels the world leading seminars for Landmark Education. He has been doing this for twelve years so it's no wonder he's confident because he gets to practise regularly.

Alain moved me and the other 100 or so people in his audience to laughter, tears, reflection, sadness and joy with the click of a tongue and a raise of an eyebrow. Sitting and watching him in wintry London for three 14-hour days and one evening was like being absorbed in a movie that you never want to end. It was real and enriching.

I asked myself how he did it. What was behind his ability to command his audience so powerfully? Sure, the content was educational and well devised but his success lay in the captivating delivery. He shared his stories with vigour and liveliness. His body language was never static. His voice travelled with passion; his eyes transmitted words; his contagious smile put us at ease.

Alain grinned endearingly. He spoke with raw guts. And the way he looked when he was speaking made me want to listen all the more. Something was magically present in his speaking that compelled us to listen.

The 59-year-old leader made us laugh again and again. No jokes, just pure wit and spontaneity. His humour was not rehearsed but flowed out of his stories. We gave him a standing ovation, and it is an event I will never forget.

Seek out the Alains of the world. Observe and learn from them. They are not concerned with ego and looking good. They take risks. Such speakers will always move us to tears because we feel that they really care about us and not about themselves.

Being a trained actor is useful because I can quickly see if someone is a fake. Alain was not. I read in one of Allan Pease's books that 'fakers can only pretend for a period of time.' I agree.

Alain also did something I have rarely seen in a male communicator. He cried. Tears fell during the sharing of a personal story that came from a place of love. Alain said he was uncomfortable about expressing his feelings but he did not hold back. The surprising effect was that he made us feel grateful that he had allowed us to watch his vulnerability. That made it even more powerful.

Naked in front of an audience

Can you imagine standing on a stage at fifteen years of age, when someone behind you accidentally stands on your trousers and they fall down? Your drama teacher is standing in the audience glaring at you with fury, your parents are in the audience and all eyes are on you.

When Rosemary came to me for coaching, she recalled how she wanted to shrivel up into a tiny ball and disappear. It has taken her tremendous courage and coaching to overcome her fear of speaking to a large audience, and she is now a spontaneous, interesting speaker. Rosemary is one of the most confident and sincere people I've ever met. Her way of overcoming her dread of public speaking was to just get out there and do it – and now people call her a natural. If only they knew!

Facing the fear monster

We overcome our fear by looking it in the face, whatever it may be. Pretending a fear doesn't exist is a sure way to make sure it does. Remember:

• Professional actors do not perform without learning their lines.

- Professional musicians must first learn to play their instruments.
- Professional speakers do not start out feeling confident about their presentations. They practise their craft, discipline themselves and manage their nervousness in front of an audience every time they perform.

School memories

My first performing memory is my debut at five years old as a daffodil in my first year of school. I was wearing a green and yellow papier-mâché costume beautifully made by my mother. I can still visualize the stalk hat sitting on my head.

A later memory reveals where my fear of speaking in public may have stemmed from. I remember sitting crying in a small dressing room backstage in a suburban public hall. I was crippled with fear, and didn't understand what was wrong with me. I was dressed as a boy holding a basket of flowers – I think I was performing in the opera *Figaro* at the time. Whatever the details, the memory of my lack of confidence is clear.

I developed into a confident teenager and, as a prefect, learnt quickly that speaking confidently in front of an assembly and class was part of the leadership role. I always felt nervous before speaking and reading prayers or excerpts from the Bible in front of the girls and nuns. But I started to feel a power that was exciting and almost addictive standing up there.

I remember practising an excerpt from Kahlil Gibran. I was around 14 years old and knew I belonged in front of an audience at that moment. The confidence wasn't always there, the nerves never went away and today as an adult I am still in that place of slight edginess and excitement as the adrenaline flows before I give a speech. Nervousness is useful – you need to have this surge of adrenaline for a great performance.

Why do we lose this inner sense of certainty years later in adulthood? I believe it's as a result of criticism and negative feedback and a lack of encouragement. I also believe it can be because something went wrong and we still hold on to those memories.

Have courage

Jazz singer, Briar Ross, has a great story about facing your fear. She explains: '*Do It Again* is my second CD, the first being *Just Do It*. That title arose from dealing with the irrational fear I had felt since a child, of speaking or performing in public. In a moment of madness I decided to do something about this fear that I felt was stopping me from being all that I could be.' After years in a successful business career, Briar decided to pursue her dream of working as a professional performer. When I saw her perform on television, I was stunned she'd overcome her lack of confidence about performing in public.

> Promise me you'll always remember: You're braver than you believe and stronger than you seem and smarter than you think.
> *Christopher Robin to Pooh, A A Milne*

I spoke with Briar about the origins of her fear of performing in public. She recalls: 'I was paralysed with fear about speaking in front of an audience. I realized where it came from. I had stuffed up a piano recital when I was seven years old. I invited my mother to listen to me sing as an adult and said to her, "Mum, it doesn't matter if I stuff up, does it?" "Yes it does," said my mother. "I remember when you mucked up when you were seven years old playing for a teacher's recital."'

Briar went on to say the audience loved her and at that moment she felt free. 'I kept doing it. Just do it,' she said with pride and confidence.

When did you lose your nerve about speaking in front of others? Who gave you the confidence to speak out? Share your stories to help others. You are not alone if you are struggling with this lack of confidence. Start talking about these memories while you are reading this book. You'll be amazed to hear many extraordinary stories that will make you realize we are all the same.

> Success consists of going from failure to failure without loss of enthusiasm.
> *Winston Churchill*

You can improve your confidence by practising your speaking and increasing your knowledge about how to present. Eloquence is something you learn. Learning self-confidence in public speaking is no different from learning to play a musical instrument or a sport.

We'll look at many of these suggestions in greater detail throughout the book, but here are my top ten points for improving your confidence in your public-speaking ability.

1. Believe in yourself
The audience will believe you if you show them you're confident and comfortable in front of them. To appear confident you need to believe in yourself and in what you are saying. Be positive. Affirm yourself – use positive self-talk. Gather a record of successful experiences.

I have observed people's body language over the years and

have noticed that business professionals who appear confident from the outside tend to be promoted, gain a second interview and command respect, more so than those who don't.

Tell yourself you are worth listening to, and enjoy the moment when the audience applauds.

2. Share true stories that will change other people's lives

Don't play it safe – empower your audience, stimulate change in the mind of your listener. Tell your own personal and professional story. If the audience can relate to your anecdotes, they feel less alone and may take away new strategies to help them deal with their problems. Start taking risks with the content of your speeches in front of non-threatening audiences.

3. Plan and prepare well in advance

Procrastination is a killer. Take time to do the necessary research before writing your speech. Do a little every day, even if it's just jotting down a few notes. Leaving preparation to the last minute will make you stressed, and the speech won't be as good as it could be. If you procrastinate, ask yourself why. Have you put the speech in the too-hard basket? If your excuse is you're too busy, why did you agree to give the speech at all? If you truly are too busy to prepare properly (and it's not just an excuse) consider asking someone else to do the speech instead.

Winston Churchill estimated it took him six to eight hours to prepare a forty-five-minute speech. Serious speakers need to set aside at least forty-five to sixty minutes of preparation time per minute of speaking time. I spend at least one to two full days preparing for a one-hour speech, and once spent four days preparing for a major speech, including practising in front of a friend to increase my confidence.

I remember working with Shelly, a client who was offered a second interview in the US for a directorship. She had an anxiety attack during her first interview, blushing, sweating and shaking. She hyperventilated and was disappointed in herself.

We rehearsed for six weeks leading up to the second interview. The difference was remarkable. She presented clearly and calmly, and was a different woman. What transformed her performance was the inner confidence that came from knowing her material inside and out.

She emailed me after the interview: 'My interview happened from 1.45 to 4.15 p.m. and was a tribute to the power of rehearsal. I felt a bit shaky in the half-hour I had to wait past my designated interview starting time, but once the presentation was underway I felt great. You won't believe this – I've never seen it in any interview before but the committee clapped at the end of the interview.'

As the saying goes, it's not about practice making perfect, it's about perfect practice making perfect performance.

4. Know what your key messages are

What ideas do you want your audience to remember from your speech? Write them down and memorize them. You can then weave these key messages into your storytelling. Know your material inside out. You're the expert. Keep things simple, and be concise.

5. Rehearse in front of a colleague or friend you respect

Confidence is not something to be plucked out of the air. It comes from knowing your performance is solid because you have proof. You've rehearsed it until it runs easily and you've had the approval of colleagues whose judgement you value.

Have a complete run-through. A rehearsal is vital for your

self-confidence. A warm-up is essential to make your body feel more alive. Breathe, move, and exercise your voice. Sports teams practise before the big day – think of mastering this craft as you would approach learning a sport.

It's very simple – if you don't rehearse, your speech will not be all it could be, and you won't have had the opportunity to discover any unexpected problems before the big day.

CRASHING ON THE DAY

The Apprentice is an entertaining reality-TV programme and good to watch as a study in presentation. In it candidates compete to win the position of an apprentice in business magnet Sir Alan Sugar's company. (In America Donald Trump is the business guru.)

You have an opportunity to see people improve and become more confidant as the weeks go on. During the last episode in the 2008 series Lee, one of the final candidates, started to crack under the pressure of having to make a presentation later in the day.

His negative dialogue dragged me away from cooking dinner, forced me onto the couch to watch the scenario play out and later write about it.

'I can't do this right now,' Lee cried out. 'I'm not ready . . . I can't do it . . . I'm doing it to myself – everything's at stake.'

Sir Alan judged him as cracking under the pressure; as he put it, 'thinking of throwing the towel in'.

What I saw was a man out of his comfort zone because he was attempting to learn a script which seemed like it had been written by committee. (Note to us all: only actors are used to learning lines quickly and can really make someone else's words seem real.)

Lee had fallen into the classic trap of living into other people's descriptions of himself (even Sir Alan told him 'your weakness is presenting') and on cue his mind started to blank with fear.

Lee's scenario brings up many issues. How do you recover from a meltdown and crisis in confidence to take the stage, podium or in Lee's case, the TV studio with an audience of millions?

Here are my sacred six tips for Lee or anyone who finds himself in such a paralysing position.

1. Don't learn your lines by rote
Lee was confidant, spontaneous, warm and relaxed when he was delivering an off-the-cuff sales pitch about underpants, able to make a compelling argument with ease. But reciting a set script made him stilted. In throwing the script away, he could have reached his peak performance.

2. Be on message
What are you saying? I advise clients to know exactly what their top three messages or bullet points are. What are the three things you want the audience to take away with them? Trust that you will be able to put it into your own words eloquently.

3. Create a storyboard
If learning lines is unavoidable and you are finding it difficult, one technique is to literally draw a picture for every element in the story. Even stick figures are fine and will stay in your mind. Learn the ideas and the words will follow.

4. Take on a character
If you're frozen with fear, take on the role of someone who isn't. Imagine a winning character and behave like that person. Act like you're ready by smiling, looking relaxed and standing straight.

5. Actively stop your negative thoughts
If the negative dialogue in your head is crippling you, use the technique of thought stopping as outlined in Chapter 11.

6. Warm up
Before going on, do a decent warm up as outlined in Chapter 8. Apart from anything it takes your mind off your own obsessive miserable thoughts.

Had I had time to coach Lee McQueen prior to his TV appearance I would have spent time alone with him with a white-board working on his negative thoughts months before the presentation. The limiting story in his head had been, I imagine, something like, 'I am not good enough. I did not go to university. I lied on TV about this,' and so on.

I would teach him how to replace these thoughts with positive short phrases. I would stand in front of him and explain that he was sabotaging his work. He would read Chapter 11 on Transforming your Fears with Self-Belief and bring his own concerns to the table after which we would follow the process through.

Later I would rehearse him with a camera and play it back over and over asking him to critique himself before receiving my feedback.

As it happens Lee became the winning candidate; so in the end he was able to turn it around. Ultimately I think the qualities that made him a winner were his positive attitude, good manners, sex appeal and joy (we are drawn to joyful people) and the fact that Sir Alan just liked him.

I coached a woman for the same programme in another country and watched her confidence increase in our rehearsals. I did a mock up of the programme using tough interviews with a real businessman to interrogate her. It stopped her from being fazed when she faced the television scenarios. Forewarned is forearmed.

Don't load yourself with the burden of turning into a Lincoln or JFK. You're rehearsing to familiarize yourself with the experience and to test out some really mundane things. Is the microphone at the right height for you? (Remember the Queen's address in June 2008 to George Bush during his final State visit and all we could see on our television screens was a talking hat in frame.)

Rehearse in the shoes you're going to be wearing. How far from the microphone should you stand? How loud should you talk? This is your chance to iron out any little things that could put you off during your real presentation.

6. Seek out and accept training opportunities

Don't wait for a really important speech to practise your public speaking. If you can try out your skills in presentations where you're relaxed about the outcome, you'll be better equipped to handle the big speeches. Presentation-skills courses abound – make the most of them as they provide instant feedback, and help to build your confidence and self-esteem.

7. Be well informed about world events and read the newspaper every day

This will expand your knowledge and vocabulary. One friend read the entire dictionary when he was a child and it shows in his use of language even today. Keep notes of anecdotes for your speeches. Refer to current issues so your audience can see that you are educated and well informed. I collect newspaper articles and file them under specific headings as a resource. I also keep a hard copy of every speech I've made.

8. Find a mentor

I was fortunate to receive an excellent education from nuns who were nurturing and serious about mentoring their students. I somehow knew at an early age I would be a successful woman in life despite many childhood setbacks.

A strong-willed fiery Irish nun, Sister Roger, was the most influential person in my childhood. She was the head of my primary and intermediate schools, and she encouraged my passion for drama and created speaking opportunities for me so I could express my creativity. I remember her telling me I was talented and to never give up on my dreams. All you need is one person in those early years to guide you through the confusion and help you to grow more confident. Everyone needs someone to believe in their talent.

9. Fake it till you make it

If you're lacking in confidence, simply pretend you're not. Project confidence even if you don't feel it inside. Move and stand with poise even if you're feeling awkward. Over the years I've learnt to act as if I'm confident even though I might be shaking in my boots. After a while, you start to feel as though you are the confident person you're pretending to be. Show your confidence to your audience through both your voice and your body language. I used to attend tap-dance classes when I ran the Performing Arts School. I was hopeless at it but loved the adrenaline and the buzz. I used to smile and pretend I was confident – no one noticed (except the teacher I'm sure) but believing I could do it kept me returning week after week to keep fit and have fun.

Wendy's first phone call and email were like many I have received – she was suffering from anxiety attacks prior to speaking in public. She had successfully managed to avoid speaking in public for years in her job but had now decided it was time to face up to her fears. She approached her boss, who supported her by making an investment in her training.

I was astonished to see how much presence she had in her first session, even though she couldn't see this quality in herself. She was subconsciously putting on a great act even though she was terrified inside. Now she believes in herself, she's able to give presentations to her team with more courage and confidence. She still has the odd nervous attack but is able to manage her nerves with breathing techniques and positive self-talk.

10. Watch star speakers

Anita Roddick was speaking at an international hotel many years back. She was passionate, enthusiastic and inspiring. Her confidence and commitment were extraordinary. She had no notes and used a polished slide presentation consisting of photos.

Nelson Mandela spoke at the same hotel a few years later to a packed room. His presence sent shivers up my spine. I remember him coming off the stage and walking toward the hotel staff to shake their hands. He walked with an air of confidence, so calm and sure of himself. He was so humble and reached out to everyone with his spirit. He engaged his audience from the beginning to the end. He had presence and his humanity touched us.

Glenda Jackson was invited to be a guest speaker to raise funds for a museum. She stood on an empty stage with no notes or props, and entertained us for an hour with her life story. I could have sat there for another three hours – her humour and passion mesmerized the audience. Her ability to communicate with ease was exceptional.

Dr John Demartini is an inspiring life coach and speaker who visits the UK at least twice a year from the USA. I have seen him three times in action in London. Watching talent like his live or on the internet is a good vehicle to learn about presence and charisma.

Others in that genre that you can learn from include Anthony Robbins, Christopher Howard and Katie Byron.

Bill Clinton is an outstanding public speaker, one of the best I've seen. I sat on the marketing advisory board of CureKids, an organization that raises funds for research into childhood life-threatening diseases, and was honoured to sit at a table with Clinton, who was fundraising on their behalf. I was excited to hear and see an experienced speaker of his calibre. I noticed the following things about his presentation:

- He exudes confidence, warmth and self-esteem.
- He uses lots of anecdotes to get his point across, especially

poignant stories and images which stay in your mind.
- His smile is friendly and genuine, and he looked happy to be there.
- He definitely has a 'presence', and seemed down to earth and relaxed.
- For the audience, it was like listening to a friend who made you feel special.
- His speech was delivered at a good pace – not too fast or slow.
- While he had notes at hand, he knew his material well and didn't use them.

Many clients also attended his presentation, and we all said the same things: Clinton has charisma. If he's ever looking for work, he could set up his own public-speaking academy.

TIPS ON DEVELOPING SELF-CONFIDENCE

Believe in yourself – you are unique. The audience will believe in you if you believe in you.

Share stories that will change other people's lives. Don't play it safe – empower your audience, stimulate change in the mind of the listener. Tell your story.

Plan and prepare well in advance. Procrastination is a killer. Take time to research and do your homework. Your preparation shows you are committed. Always debrief with a colleague, get feedback.

Respect yourself more. Speak positively to and about yourself.

Hold on to the memory of the last successful speech you gave. Focus on that one, not the one that you associate with failure.

Know what your key messages are, write them down and memorize them.

Rehearse in front of a colleague and friend you respect. Have a complete run-through. A rehearsal is vital for your self-confidence.

A warm-up is essential to make your body feel more alive. Breathe, move, and vocalize. Five minutes is better than nothing.

Be positive. Affirm yourself – use positive self-talk. Get a record of successful experiences behind you.

Know your material inside and out. You are the expert. If you don't know your subject matter, don't give the presentation. Speak from the heart.

2

BRAIN POWER

Intellectual growth should commence at birth and cease only at death.
Albert Einstein

The brain is your body's control centre. If you look after it and understand how it functions, you can help it to work better, and your public speaking and general wellbeing will improve as a result.

We use about 5 per cent of our brain on our usual day-to-day tasks. What do we do with the rest? We use our mind to focus, think, and communicate, so it's important to understand how to use it to its full potential. Imagine how much more we could achieve when writing or delivering speeches if we could only harness a little more of that latent brainpower.

People who experience nervousness or stage fright before speaking in public benefit from understanding the chemical reactions taking place in their mind and body when they are under stress. Over the years clients have commented on how useful it is to understand how the brain functions when they are standing in front of an audience, because it makes them less afraid.

As an actor, I was more afraid of my mind going blank and forgetting my lines than anything else. Now that I understand more about the workings of the brain I'm able to trust I'll remember my material. Practise some of the exercises in this chapter and you will start to feel more focused and confident in your presentations. As Laurence Olivier once said, 'It is natural to be nervous, but it is an art not to show it.'

Understanding your brain

Gordon Dryden and Dr Jeanette Vos, in *The Learning Revolution*, refer to the brain as the world's finest computer. This book is a masterpiece of research and brings together some of the twentieth century's finest scholars on learning and the brain. I recommend this book if you are interested in learning in detail about the wonderful workings of the brain and how they can be applied to your style of learning. Understanding more about how the brain works can help you to identify how you best process information.

Roger Sperry received the Nobel Prize in 1981 for his groundbreaking work in brain research, particularly in the field of left- and right-brain theory. He found that the human brain has specialized functions on the left and right, and that the two sides of the brain can operate independently. Professor Ornstein of the University of California further researched this phenomenon, reported in *Make the Most of Your Mind* by Tony Buzan, and concluded that the following types of mental activities are activated by the left brain:

- logic
- lists
- linearity
- words
- numbers
- sequence
- analysis

While the right side of the brain handles activities such as:

- rhythm
- colour
- imagination
- daydreaming
- dimension
- spatial awareness
- music

We all use both our left and right brains, but tend to emphasize one over the other. I'm definitely more right-brain-orientated than left, for example. My teachers often said, 'Margaret needs to concentrate more.' Daydreaming helps with problem solving and creative thinking – I simply needed a more creative approach to my studies. And yet I would come top in theology because I was fascinated with ideas and loved to debate.

In contrast, one of my brothers, Tony, is very left-brain and gifted, coming top of the school in his exams. He is now a successful chartered accountant with an extraordinary appreciation of the visual arts. I'm sure that being raised by a father who worked as an accounts clerk during the day and a visual artist at night and in the weekends contributed to our family's eclectic nature.

What about you? Can you identify whether you are more left- or right-brain-oriented?

What is stage fright?

The dictionary defines 'fright' as 'sudden or extreme fear'. Going blank in front of an audience is certainly terrifying. Why could you remember your material when practising at home, but not when delivering the presentation? Stress induced by being in front of an audience can trigger a chemical process in your brain, affecting your memory. This occurs for many people when they stand up in front of a crowd.

In the case of my friend Giulia Sirignani, an Australian television broadcaster and journalist who has worked for both the Australian Broadcasting Corporation and Channel 9, it wasn't a real audience that triggered a blank, but an estimated television audience of a million people. She'd been doing live reports from the Vatican in Rome three times a day for months on end to cover the death of Pope John Paul II in 2005. She and the network had been happy with her performance, and her self-confidence and esteem were in good shape. Then 'disaster struck', as she recalls it:

'It was the day after the world had learned that Joseph Ratzinger had been elected as the next Pope. I was asked to do a live introduction to my story on the evening news and while I was waiting in our position at the Vatican for the newsreader to introduce me, I suddenly started to get really, really nervous. I was extremely tired after months of very little sleep and was feeling a little distracted because of a lot of movement on the set around me, but when I heard my count-down from the studio in Sydney, "ten, nine, eight, seven . . .", my heart started racing and for no apparent reason I felt terrified. I'd been doing this every day, and I've been in TV for nearly 15 years, so why the sudden panic attack? I started to talk but heard a noise off-camera and at that point I went completely blank and forgot what I was saying. It was the lowest point in my career. All attempts at consolation and assurances that "it happens to everyone in their career" didn't move me one bit. I still shudder when I think of the longest three seconds of my life!'

What causes stage fright?
Your brain makes 100,000 chemical reactions per second and consists of 100 billion neurons or active nerve cells. These nerve cells are located in the outer layer of the cortex. An

active human brain can generate 10 watts of electricity, and weighs approximately 1.4 kilograms.

Dinah Bradley, author of *Hyperventilation Syndrome*, says, 'Our visual sense operates mainly in the larger area of the brain. No one has worked out why, but our brains don't differentiate between vividly imagined events and real ones. When you think about a painful or frightening situation, your body reacts as if it's actually happening.'

The solution? If you experience stage fright, first of all, don't worry. Try to centre yourself and allow your brain to kick in and bring you back to your thoughts. You'll be OK. You're not losing your mind or suffering from early dementia.

About two billion brain cells make up our speech and thought centres.
Dinah Bradley

Remember to breathe deeply and stay calm. The words will come. If they don't, ask the audience to help you. If I lose my words when teaching, I often say, 'Where was I now?' or I turn to my co-presenter and ask for help. Trust that someone will rescue or assist you – people want to help. Don't judge yourself. What seems like a lifetime to you is a few seconds to the audience. They are on your side and do not want you to fail.

The stress reaction

Dr Gail Ratcliffe is a clinical psychologist specializing in the diagnosis and management of stress. I recommend her book, *Take Control of your Life*, if you would like to know more about the effects of stress on your body. She describes the changes that happen in your brain and body when you are experiencing stress as a cycle, which has four stages:

1. Negative thoughts, such as 'I am too scared to give this speech.'
2. Emotions, such as anxiety, arising from the negative thoughts.
3. Chemical reactions in your body. The negative thoughts send nerve impulses to the adrenal gland on your kidneys, which speeds up the action of many organs and triggers the release of a number of different chemicals into your blood stream.
4. Physical symptoms occur as a result, such as sweaty palms, churning stomach or a thumping heart. Physical symptoms vary from person to person. The physical symptoms also manifest in the brain, dilating the arteries, which can cause headaches in some people. It also makes it difficult to think clearly and to remember. The stress chemicals actually interfere with the neural transmission, making it harder for the brain to understand the messages it receives.

Dr Georgi Lozanov, a Bulgarian physician, psychiatrist and educational researcher, is highly recognized for his 25-year contribution to the field of accelerated learning. He suggests that our subconscious attitudes limit our perception about what is real or possible. Lozanov suggests that our limiting attitudes result largely from childhood conditioning and that these form learning barriers. If you believe you can't successfully speak in public, you'll kickstart the stress reaction and have trouble preparing and delivering your speech.

The effects of stress

Do you ever get headaches before you make a speech or when you are stressed? I've experienced stress headaches before a speech when under pressure, and over the years I've seen many clients suffer from headaches in public-speaking workshops. This is a normal reaction when you are frightened or stressed.

One client, Diane, experienced extreme stress when preparing for a presentation. She had to deliver a speech to a group of secondary-school students, and had been up all night worrying. On the day of the presentation, she felt ill and had a headache. Her brain felt as though it was exploding. She nearly turned the car around and thought about calling the organizer to say she couldn't make it. She went ahead with the presentation, which was successful, but she didn't feel confident and doubted her abilities.

I asked her many questions when we talked about that morning and was surprised that her stress levels became so high every time she was out of her comfort zone. Diane felt embarrassed and angry with herself. She had to learn to cease this self-criticism, and she realized she had to face her fear. She was terrified because she felt out of control. I reassured her that her story was common and her physical reactions a normal consequence of feeling so stressed. Knowing that she could learn to control the stress reaction was a big step in the right direction.

Diane's stress hormones and chemicals were interfering with the action of her neural transmitters. They affected her brain chemistry so it was difficult for her to think clearly and make rational decisions. It was a physical impossibility for Diane to be at her best intellectually when she was so stressed. Her brain was simply not able to operate properly.

Exercises to reduce the effects of stress
Breathing
Find a quiet place where you won't be distracted or feel inhibited. It could be in your hotel room or car, or even a toilet cubicle. Close your eyes for five minutes, sitting with a straight spine. Take slow, deep breaths, focusing on the flow of the breath in and out of your lungs. Relax your head, shoulders and arms. Let go of all the tension in your body. Clear your mind of clutter. Visualize a gentle breeze taking away all the muddled thoughts preventing your mind from relaxing.

Positive self-talk
Say to yourself: 'I am calm, I am in control, I am ready to speak with ease.' Repeat this over and over, sending a positive message to your brain.

Ask for help
Call a friend or colleague you trust, and ask them for help. Ask them to talk you through your fear and to help calm you down. Even the process of putting the problem into words is a positive step. Speaking about the issue is a constructive way to solve the problem, not an admission of failure. If Diane had called me before her speech, I would have reminded her of her expertise in her field and asked her to believe in herself.

Cross crawling
'Cross crawling' is a well-known accelerated-learning exercise and easy to do before a presentation. Tap your left hand to your right knee in front of your body, and then repeat with your right hand and left knee. Next, repeat the sequence, this time with your arms and feet meeting behind your body. This exercise aims to integrate the left meridian of the brain with the right, and helps to relax your mind. You could think

of a different activity that involves thinking and using both sides of your body – for example, you could juggle balls before a speech. It also takes your focus off your fear and gets the blood moving.

Looking after your brain

> Hope, enthusiasm and wisdom are to the mind as food is to the body.
> *Dadi Janki*

Thinking and memory are chemical processes. Look after your brain and you'll find speaking in public becomes easier – because you're focused, alert and ready for action. These are the main areas in which only a little effort will significantly enhance your brain's performance.

Oxygen

Lack of oxygen makes you drowsy and lethargic, and can cause memory loss. Have a window open if you can. Unfortunately, many of us work in high-rise buildings with air conditioning, so make an effort to leave the office during every day to refresh yourself and get a good supply of oxygen to your brain. Oxygen helps you to think more clearly and be more creative in meetings. Before you give an important presentation get some fresh air, even if you step outside for just a few minutes. I make a habit of going for a quick walk in between meetings to give me a boost so I am refreshed and alert. Even five minutes makes a difference to how you feel. You will think more clearly, be more alert and deliver with more energy.

Restful sleep

Feeling nervous the night before a big presentation is completely normal behaviour. Go to bed earlier than usual the night before, or even the week before presenting. Getting enough sleep seems so obvious, but it makes such a difference. We are more awake and positive when we get plenty of deep, relaxed sleep.

I see many people sitting up late the night before a speech, because they have procrastinated about their preparation. We've all been there, myself included. If you find yourself in this position, learn from your experience and don't put yourself in this situation again. If you're over-tired, you won't be able to perform at your best. Restful sleep will help you more in the long run than typing up your notes or rehearsing till late the night before. So hit the hay when you know the outcome is important.

If you have trouble sleeping, try the following suggestions:

- Lavender oil in a warm bath or on a pillow is good for relaxation.
- A cup of warm milk can encourage sleep.
- Try the breathing exercises discussed earlier.
- Turn off the television well before you go to bed.
- Listen to soothing music.
- Use earplugs to shut out all noise.

Brain food

Eat good, clean, healthy food before any speech to maintain your energy levels. Studies have shown that the intake of food is associated with an increase in blood levels of B-endorphins, an important vitamin for optimum brain functioning. Carrots are rich in vitamin B – get into the habit of taking fresh carrots to work to munch on. In general, aim to maintain a balanced diet by eating lots of fresh food, including at least five portions of fresh fruit and vegetables every day.

> One cannot think well, love well, and sleep well, if one has not dined well.
> *Virginia Woolf*

Naturopath Bill McKay is a great believer in eating regularly to avoid tiredness. I was eating well but not often enough and wondered why I lacked energy when leading a one-day public-speaking seminar. My memory was not as good as it could be so I asked Bill for his advice. With his guidance I started to snack or 'graze' on low-fat brain food throughout the day like almonds, which are rich with protein. No more mid-afternoon chocolate bars! Changing my eating habits has made an enormous difference to my energy levels and memory retention.

According to life-skills coach Clive Littin, 'it takes 28 days to change a habit.' Once you've managed a new way of doing things for a month, it'll be as if you've being doing it forever. So if eating healthily is a new challenge for you, buy healthy snack food and carry it in your briefcase, handbag or even your pocket! Store it in an airtight jar on your desk and get into the habit of reaching for your healthy stash every couple of hours. I've been caught without snacks on the odd occasion and given a speech on an empty stomach, and felt low in energy as a result. Your brain helps your thoughts to flow when it has enough fuel.

Fluids

Drink at least six glasses of water a day. Your brain's weight is more then 70 per cent water, and if it becomes dehydrated, you'll feel tired and headachy. I have days when I don't drink enough water and, sure enough, a headache soon appears. If I drink at least six glasses my thinking is much sharper.

Keep coffee and tea to a minimum before speeches as they force your kidneys to excrete fluids from your body. I was so nervous when I first hit the speaking circuit, I drank endless cups of coffee in my hotel room beforehand and then wondered why I was speedy, headachy and always running to the loo!

It's no surprise that alcohol should also be avoided before presentations. While it may give you a false sense of confidence, it will also slow your brain and dull your perceptions, which are crucial when presenting. Consider whether you could reduce your alcohol intake – your brain will thank you for it.

Exercise your body . . . and your brain

Walking is free and a wonderful way of taking care of your brain. Most therapists recommend that their clients exercise to prevent burnout. We are nicer people to be around when we exercise because of the release of endorphins in our bodies. These amino acids are natural painkillers and elevate our moods, which is why we feel good after exercise.

It's easier said than done, but try to make exercise an important priority in your life – you'll appreciate the benefits.

Stimulate your brain

The more I read, go to the movies and plays, exercise, meditate, teach, study, write and partake in intellectual discussions, the more my brain is stimulated. Don't allow yourself to become bored with life or let your brain become lazy. It is an organ that needs feeding and stimulation. My father retired in his sixties, and quickly became bored with his daily routine.

I noticed a real change in his energy and outlook on life. He ended up returning to the workforce to gain the stimulation he needed to maintain a healthy brain.

> Your brain can keep learning from birth till the end of life.
> *Marian Diamond, University of California, Berkeley*

Music

According to studies, some music stimulates the brain. Some people find that listening to non-lyrical music is relaxing and helps them to concentrate on a focused mental activity.

Think of certain music as sound energy to motivate and stir the brain. Over the years I have come to realize that specific music has a profound effect on my brain and creates wellbeing in my life and in the lives of others. When I worked in an open-plan environment, a consultant often used to say, 'Who needs some music?' If we were feeling tired, the music would uplift our spirits and put smiles on our faces. Go to a symphony orchestra concert or listen to classical music and you will notice the profound effect the sounds have on you. You will feel more positive and energetic.

Aromatherapy

Consider trying aromatherapy to help sharpen your memory skills – rosemary and basil essential oils are good for improving memory. A colleague once set up a burner with aromatherapy oils near her desk; the scent was exquisite. She also used lavender oil for relaxation before presentations. Visit an aromatherapist if you want more information or seek advice from books and friends.

Most of us think about these things but we are sometimes

too shy about standing out in the work environment in case we are judged. Stand tall and be yourself – you'll set a great example for the others in your workplace.

TIPS ON USING YOUR BRAIN

Stress is a chemical reaction that occurs in your brain – you can learn to control your reaction to stressful situations.

Your brain is a wonderful organ that deserves to be looked after. Do all you can to keep it in good health, and you'll be rewarded through increased mental alertness.

Your thoughts become reality – think positive thoughts both before and during your presentation. Visualize a successful outcome to your speech.

Successful public speaking involves quick thinking and energy to communicate ideas effectively to your audience. Paying attention to your health will help you to deliver a great presentation.

3

BODY LANGUAGE

It's how you looked when you said it, not what you actually said.
Allan and Barbara Pease, The Definitive Book of Body Language

Your body language tells the audience exactly what you're thinking – whether you're happy to be there, nervous, bored or terrified. It tells them far more than the words you actually speak. If you are aware of your body language, you can make sure its message is what you mean it to be. This chapter will give you simple guidelines to help you better communicate your authenticity to your audience.

What the experts say

There are 750,000 body language signals of which about 1,500 different signals can be identified from facial movements and expressions alone.

Sociolinguist Albert Mehrabian, well known for his studies of nonverbal communication, discovered that 55 per cent of your presentation's impact is determined by body language, 38 per cent by your voice and only 7 per cent by the words you use. The exact percentages vary from study to study, but the message is the same: effective body language is crucial to the success of your speech.

When I introduce these statistics to clients they often react with surprise or disbelief. Why? Because a large percentage of our messages comes from something we may not even be aware of.

Body language determines the outcome of your communication. This is not to say the messages you are speaking about are not important; they are vital. But body language tells us a lot about how you are feeling and can distract the audience from the key messages if you are nervous or lacking confidence. Effective body language allows the audience to concentrate on what you are saying without distraction.

Why does body language matter?

Consider these two contrasting examples. Theatre director Mary Amoore recalls a story about Laurence Olivier when he was performing in a play in London in the 1960s. She was in the audience and his eyes met hers when he entered the stage. She felt special and honoured, and felt as though he had connected with her.

Not long after hearing this story, I attended a business dinner party where I sat next to a chief executive who slouched in his chair with hunched shoulders. His body language was almost child-like and lacking in confidence. The next day one of the other dinner guests commented about his body language, saying, 'He doesn't look like a chief executive.' He formed an opinion based on what he saw. People do judge on first encounters.

Like it or not, we assess people within thirty seconds of meeting them. We are not always consciously aware of reading nonverbal messages but we do it every day. That's why it's important to get the fundamentals right with your public speaking – your message is not only the words you say. Your body language will engage or isolate an audience, who will respond both consciously and subconsciously to what your body is 'saying' to them. Every time you deliver a speech or present in a meeting you are communicating nonverbally. It is impossible to make a neutral statement.

You can learn to improve your body language

A good game I recommend to those who want to hone their body language awareness is to take yourself to a public space and really observe the people or players before you. Guess the emotion they are going through.

A good place for this, where you get the whole range of emotions – grief, elation, sadness, desperation, frustration, exhaustion, love and longing – is Heathrow Airport. When next you find yourself at an airport waiting for a flight, take a good look around you and perfect your skill in reading the body's language.

Not many people are born natural public speakers. We learn as we make mistakes and progress as we receive feedback, improving with practice and by applying simple techniques.

Who you are speaks so loudly that I can't hear what you're saying.
Ralph Waldo Emerson

My first learning experience about body language was when a university invited me to address a group of scientists in the early 1980s. I wanted to decline the invitation because I wasn't experienced at speaking to an academic audience. Marilyn Waring, a politician at the time, encouraged me to accept the challenge. With her coaching I wrote a speech on education in the twenty-first century. Her background as a trained opera singer showed me the importance of correct body language. However, fear got in the way during the speech and I clung to the podium, resting my chin on one hand, with my right elbow glued to the podium. The start was shaky and my body language showed the audience how nervous I was. As the speech progressed, I decided to be myself, relax, be spontaneous and move away from behind the lectern. I moved closer to the audience and eventually performed with passion and enthusiasm.

I learnt more about the pitfalls of distracting body language that day than any other. Fear had kept me behind the lectern and, while I was there, the audience could only see a talking head. My overriding thought was, 'I am afraid you will not like this.' I committed that day to improving my public-speaking skills.

Feedback is crucial

The frustrating thing about improving your own body language is that it's very difficult to be constantly aware of how you are coming across. Usually presenters are so focused on delivering the words they're not aware of whether their arms are folded across their chest, giving them a defensive air, or if they're wringing their hands and appearing nervous.

My preference is to film clients when helping them with their public-speaking skills. This way, the clients can clearly see for themselves what looks great, and what isn't working. The film can be replayed, and compared with other perform-ances. I strongly suggest you borrow, hire or buy a digital camera and ask a friend or colleague to record a rehearsal. When I first began to give presentations, I hired an experi-enced actor to film me once a week to help analyse and improve my performance skills. When I look at the tapes now I cringe at my lack of confidence at the time, but it's great to think how much I have improved. You don't have to hire an expert – a technically astute friend or colleague is sure to be able to record your performance.

If it isn't possible to use technology, it is still worth asking for feedback during rehearsal from your 'test audience', even if it's only one person. Even if they only notice one point about your body language, it may be the crucial thing that turns you into a star presenter.

Ask around your friends and colleagues and get feedback about speeches you gave years ago and congratulate yourself on how far you have come.

Elements of body language

Body posture

Good posture conveys a sense of personal power. The body is saying, 'I am comfortable and relaxed about being here with you.' It communicates a message of confidence.

Improve your posture by standing tall and moving naturally and easily. Keep your posture upright but still relaxed. You don't want to appear arrogant and stiff. When communicating it is more effective to be fluid than locked into a rigid position.

Maintaining good posture requires an awareness of ourselves.
Dr Tristan Roberts, formerly Reader in Physiology at the University of Glasgow

---

How you hold yourself physically can reflect how you think of yourself. How you think of yourself is usually how others will think of you. The audience tends to treat you exactly as you ask to be treated. For example, when we are happy we walk along the street with our heads up high and a smile on our faces. Our posture tells the onlookers we are feeling good about the day. Standing straight also makes you feel more in control.

Many years ago, a client came to me wondering why his colleagues told him he projected coldness and arrogance. At his first training session, he sat with his legs wide apart and his arms folded behind his head. His body language communicated, 'I think I'm better than you.'

It is my belief communication and energy cannot be separated. Be conscious of what your body is saying and doing. Is it slumping, saying, 'I am depressed and tired?' Is it saying, 'I am vibrant and in love with life?' Is it closed and defensive? Is it open and speaking to the audience with enthusiasm? Posture never deceives an audience. In working with clients I get them to observe their posture on screen so they can see for themselves when they are hunched up, lop-sided or looking awkward. I tape their performance, and it's great to see the transformation from a crunched-up diaphragm and droopy shoulders to shoulders back, chest out, spine straight, head sitting comfortably on top of the spine, looking on top of the world.

Moving around the stage

If your actions on stage are to be believable and reinforce your message, they must be natural. There also needs to be a reason for them – don't fall into the trap of moving for the sake of it. Think of wherever you're performing as a stage, be it in a boardroom, a theatre or at a family gathering.

Is there a John Wayne without that walk?
Ken Howard

Again, recording a rehearsal on camera works well because you can see if you are swaying, pacing or shifting your weight from hip to hip. Other distracting habits include bouncing up and down on your heels, and slightly lifting the lectern off the floor when leaning on it. Recording the rehearsal is the best way I know of changing old habits. As your awareness increases, you will start to move freely, expressing yourself in a more natural manner.

Each movement you make during a speech must have a purpose. I often walk towards my audience to feel closer to them, speak and move back to what I call home base – centre stage or the lectern. If you sit or stand in one place for too long, you can become stiff or rigid. Your audience will respond more if you are moving in a relaxed, coordinated way.

Ask yourself when you are next giving a speech, am I

Incorrect posture   Correct posture

moving for the sake of moving? Am I pacing because I am nervous or am I moving to point to the screen or write on the whiteboard? It's OK to be still – the audience will see this as calmness, dignity and pride. Move with grace, thought and conviction, and with your body truly connecting to your message. Be grounded.

Gesturing should help tell the story. Meaningless or repeated movement doesn't add to your presentation and may even confuse your audience because the gestures don't draw people into the narrative. Try acting out a character in a familiar story, experimenting with movement and gesturing. Working in front of a partner, try acting out the same story with inappropriate movements and analyse the effect this has on your audience.

Watch your friends and colleagues move at functions. Do they move with ease? Do they carry tension in their bodies?

Dr Geordie Jahner, PhD in Psychology, is an expert in the field of movement. She says:

'Movement, when explored consciously and with aware-ness, is an amazing tool for freeing the creative self and the creative imagination. By freeing the body, we automatically begin to free ourselves emotionally and mentally from the things that hold us back. A freely moving body exudes confi-dence and enthusiasm and allows the natural flow of our innate creative spirit. Our habitual postures, gestures and body language vividly reflect our internal states and communicate volumes to our audience. A stuck body equals a stuck self. A healthy moving body reflects a healthy moving self.'

Gestures
Natural gestures influence the way an audience looks at you and listens to you. They are organic and flow from within when we're engaged in conversation.

> You cannot shake hands with a clenched fist.
> *Indira Gandhi*

My first contact with clients is revealing because of their handshake – is it confident, aggressive or weak? A soft, floppy handshake is very off-putting and implies a lack of confidence.

A friend had the difficult task of telling her chief executive that, when he spoke to an audience, he had the habit of 'rearranging' his personal equipment. She was honest and compassionate, and used a little bit of humour while explaining that he needed to relax his hands by his sides, or clasp them in a relaxed manner. The moral of the story? Be conscious of what your hands are doing when giving a presentation.

I have always encouraged my clients to discover their own vocabulary of gestures. Gestures help to convey the message. They must be natural, expressive and clear. But they must also be spontaneous and authentic. Never use gestures for the sake of using them.

What are your habits? Ask for feedback. Your gestures will show whether you are open or closed. An audience responds to open body language, not arrogant, defensive or closed body language.

> A gesture made for its own sake has no place on the stage.
> *Constantin Stanislavski*

In a typical public-speaking workshop, peers will review each other's performances. The most critical feedback always centres on unnecessary gestures that rob the message of its impact, usually hand wringing, hair curling, pencil fondling, table tapping, ring twisting, and yes – even tie stroking. One client always used to jingle his coins in his pocket, which would distract me from what he was saying.

I never train clients to use a particular pattern of gestures, because it appears false and robotic. The more you are comfortable and relaxed in your body and passionate about your message, your natural gestures will follow the words. If you don't gesture, don't get hung up about it but do see the difference for yourself on film so you can broaden your body-language vocabulary and see how much more expressive you are when you move with your words.

When you fiddle with an earring or watch, cover your face or pick at your cuticles, you send out a message that you are tense or uncertain. Your gestures must match your words, not contradict them. If you say something one way verbally but a different way nonverbally, your audience will always believe your nonverbal message.

If you keep your hands on your hips, it implies to the audience 'I know better than you', but if you hold your arms crossed over your chest, it indicates defensive, closed body language. Alternatively, if your head leans to one side, it gives the impression that you are a victim.

When I am coaching I often turn the sound down on the TV monitor so the client can look at gestures or lack of them. For example, a speaker saying, 'It's great to be here today,' with his eyes glued to the page is actually saying the opposite, through his body language.

Practise gesturing in front of a mirror. Explore gesturing with a partner, using a familiar phrase like: 'This memory stick is my office.' Experiment with different gestures, mirroring each other's hand and arm movements. Gesture using all the space. Film your own gesturing exercise, and in doing so attempt to create a variety of gestures so that you can see which ones work – and which ones don't.

Facial expressions

Don't forget your facial expressions. An expressionless face has no credibility – it looks as if you simply do not care enough to put the effort into delivering your message. Phony smiles also give you away, while a true smile comes from within. Of course, there are times when it's not appropriate to smile, so be aware of the context of your presentation.

Whether in pictures, in film or in life, Princess Diana over the course of her royal public life mastered the power of the body's language. She transformed herself from "shy-Di" to become the most dazzling woman on the global stage.

Her youngest son, Prince Harry, has inherited her touch. Just look at how natural and at ease he appears in his body language when he is talking to children. His smile and presence even moves to tears the children he greets on a walkabout.

Eye contact

Eye contact is a crucial aspect of communication. It humanizes you and implies honesty. It shows you care and are interested in your audience, helping people to feel a part of your journey, and drawing them in.

Looking into a person's eyes helps to build a rapport with him. The eyes are the window of the soul. Looking someone in the eye is not intended to make someone feel uncomfortable – don't stare, but simply maintain eye contact for a few seconds at a time.

> There is nothing more awful than an actor with vacant eyes.
> A gesture made for its own sake has no place on the stage.
> *Constantin Stanislavski*

The pupil of the eye will dilate as a sign of approval and constrict for disapproval. We warm to people with enlarged pupils. Watch people's faces to learn about what is going on in their minds. Particularly observe changes in expression.

If the audience is too big for you to make eye contact with every person, try to make eye contact with at least a few people from different sections, including those at the back and sides of the room. When I performed at my first celebrity debate a journalist in the audience told me, 'You were wonderful but you hardly looked at the audience, you spoke to your notes too much.' The auditorium was in darkness so I had almost forgotten there was an audience present. I was grateful for her honesty even though it was upsetting. Every time you make a mistake like this, celebrate it. You will move on and improve.

If you have never worked on a stage with lights in your face and the audience in the dark, get access to a studio and rehearse in this environment. Remember to avoid looking at the ceiling, floor and walls, and practise maintaining eye contact with people.

Hints for healthy eyes
- If you wear glasses or contact lens, make sure you have them with you when presenting, and a back-up pair if necessary.
- Use drops in your eyes if they are sore.
- Put chilled cucumber slices on your eyes, and lie down for five minutes.

- Put a few drops of lavender oil on an eye pillow and place over your eyes, lying down for at least ten minutes.

The eye-contact rules:
- Never look down. Instead, maintain frequent eye contact whether you are listening or talking, but never stare.
- Embrace the audience with your eyes and keep your eyes up. Too much eye contact can give out the wrong signals such as sexual attraction, anger or challenge so give some relief by looking away every few seconds.
- The 7-second rule works for most of my clients. Look for 5–7 seconds per person or per row then move your eyes on.

Exercises to encourage natural movement
Before your presentation, loosen up your body by:
- Running or walking on the spot.
- Shaking your feet or legs one at a time.
- Shaking your whole body.

Exercises to encourage natural gestures
- Before your presentation:
- Shake your arms.
- Shake your hands and relax your fingers.
- Clench your hands and relax them, and repeat.
- Lift your shoulders up, holding them tight and still. Next, drop them gently and relax. Repeat the exercise, being aware of your breath, breathing in as you raise your shoulders and exhaling as you lower them.
- Practise delivering your speech walking around the room using gestures and then standing still but using your arms and hands. Which feels more natural?

Exercises to relax your face before a speech

- We wear our tension on the face so do at least one of these to look and feel more relaxed.
- Touch your face with your tongue – aim for your nose.
- Slowly massage your face with your hands, with your eyes closed.
- Move your tongue around in your mouth, massaging the inside of the mouth.
- Open your mouth, stretching all the muscles, eyes wide open, then close your eyes and mouth, screwing your face up. Repeat then relax.
- Blow air between your lips, like a horse.
- Laugh – it's a great tension reliever.
- Splash cold water on your face to freshen yourself up or use a natural water spray.
- The tongue twisters in the warm-up chapter will help to loosen up your face and jaw

Common body-language mistakes

Watch out for the following gestures that can distract from the power of your performance. Movement must have a purpose – otherwise it's distracting.

- hands in pockets
- hands clasped behind back
- hands nervously wringing
- hands in front of crotch (fig-leaf pose)
- touching your watch or ring
- preening your hair
- adjusting your belt, waistband or bra strap
- shuffling your feet, walking on the spot
- pointing your finger at the audience
- chin resting on hands
- touching your mouth, eye or earlobe unnecessarily

TIPS ON BODY LANGUAGE

Body language matters – every time you deliver a speech you are communicating nonverbally. It is impossible to make a neutral statement.

Be confident to move about the room, using your hands and face expressively to communicate your message.

Getting feedback is the best way to improve your body language during presentations. Filming your rehearsals is a great way to do this.

Study other people's body language so you increase your awareness and understanding.

Watch out for the unconscious gestures that can convey nervousness, especially hand wringing, fiddling with jewellery and touching your face or hair.

Record interviews from business programmes, celebrity shows, the news and documentaries, and notice the different types of body language.

4

FINDING YOUR VOICE

To free the voice is to free the person.
Kristin Linklater

Speech is thought to have developed over two million years ago. The earliest sounds were made in the throat to convey emotion. It is a joy to watch and listen to children making sounds. I was in London when my 15-month-old godson Leo said 'Maggie' for the first time. I was stunned. He had echoed me when I repeated the sounds of my name.

Why are some people more persuasive than others? Listen to the voices of people you consider persuasive, and notice how they speak. Think of your voice as an expressive musical instrument, which you can fine-tune so it sounds more convincing. Learn to look after it, use it well and enjoy it. If you speak from the heart and express ideas with enthusiasm, you and your presentation are more likely to be remembered.

Gail is a confident black woman who is a sought-after motivational speaker to business and educational audiences. She was invited to speak to a multicultural audience at a secondary school in a socially disadvantaged community. She had written a carefully structured speech about tertiary education but, after the first five minutes, she looked up from her scripted text and said, 'I cannot do this.' What she meant was that by reading her prepared talk, she felt she had lost her authentic voice. She had to stop reading and began talking without a script.

Her message was powerful. Gail shared the story of her early life. How could she tell an auditorium full of teenagers that she had been given away as a baby, raped as a fifteen-year-old and had hung out with motorbike gangs? But this brave woman gave herself permission to open up to a crowd of strangers, even though her voice was shaking and deep inside something was saying, 'this is a nightmare'.

'My emotion was very present because I was speaking the truth,' she said. 'I gave a twenty-minute speech off the cuff.' In her talk she said: 'Look at me, look at my remuneration, it is in the top one per cent of earners in this country. You can do this too. It is only the value you place on your self-worth that limits your potential. I had an instinct and I acted on it.'

When you harness your feelings your voice is more powerful. Are you afraid your voice will quiver, break, fall away with emotion if you raise personal issues? Do you think this invalidates your argument? There is a difference between harnessing your personal experiences and 'spilling your guts'. Be brave like Gail. Seize the moment to connect with your audience.

Linda Cartwright is a top voice coach who I've worked with for over 15 years. She says, 'Forget about the eyes being the windows to the soul – it's the voice! I do believe you are what you speak. I also believe anyone can speak in a way which simply and directly communicates not just information to listeners but also the fact that they are a trustworthy person who carries great authority and to whom it would be advisable to listen. You can make people want to listen to you. Remember, your audience will spend so much time worrying about you if you appear to be nervous that they won't take in what you're saying. They will go to sleep if you sound boring. They will doubt you if you sound hesitant.'

You can learn to sound more relaxed, confident and assertive by simply being yourself and by practising a few of the straightforward exercises in this chapter. You may also like to spend time with a professional voice coach to keep up the good work. If you decide to do further research into how to use your voice effectively, I recommend reading *Freeing the Natural Voice* by Kristin Linklater and *The Right to Speak* by Patsy Rodenburg.

Putting passion in your voice

Before getting technical with clients about their voices, I try to teach them how to sound more passionate. If your voice is flat, you sound depressed or bored, regardless of how you actually feel. When we are happy we sound more passionate; when we are turned on to life we have zing and energy in our voices. Passion is not about technique. You have to find a reason to get fired up about the presentation you're preparing for, as faking passion is easy to spot. Passion is a very strong emotion that contains enthusiasm and feeling, and it is hard to convey this emotion when you are stressed, tired or overworked.

If you know your subject matter inside out, and you are enthusiastic when expressing your ideas, you will sound convincing and passionate. Your voice reflects your thoughts and feelings. Words by themselves are not enough; we need our audience to believe us.

Remember, it's not just about selling an idea or a concept in a presentation; it's about the excitement behind the thought or idea. When the Performing Arts School needed a large amount of sponsorship in order to launch Theatresports, targeting one keen sponsor with an interest in the arts made sense. The television producer and I made a heartfelt presentation and walked away with the signed contract. Later I asked the sponsor at a cocktail party what it was that had persuaded him to endorse Theatresports. He looked at me and said, 'Maggie, it was because of your passion and belief.' I was taken aback by his response. We had screamed with joy in the lift on the way back down from his office … and he'd heard us! He said our enthusiasm and passion for the product was contagious.

One client I worked with was given feedback by his boss that his voice was quiet and lacked passion and, therefore, his leadership style was affected. He was also told he was too quiet. After several months of coaching he started to let go of his inhibitions and his voice is now more powerful and confident. This manager had a breakthrough when he realized he had to get in touch with his emotions in order to express the real him. There was nothing wrong with the sound of his voice. He just couldn't always be heard; he didn't project his voice sufficiently. He was afraid to let his passion out.

Another client started to share stories which meant a great deal to him during a training session one day. This allowed him to connect with his heart. He was raised in a third-world country where the culture influenced him to be very polite, quietly spoken and, according to him, 'seen and not heard'. When he began to project his voice, his subject matter was more engaging – it was because of the passion behind the words. And yet, when he was giving a work-focused presentation, his performance was flat and lacked this enthusiasm.

Understanding that he needed to emotionally connect with his material means that he now presents confidently with strength and projection in his voice in front of politicians, local government audiences and professionals. He realizes he is a better presenter when he is himself and trusts in his voice. He didn't need to adopt a particular voice technique, but rather give himself permission to release his passion. It is often emotional issues that keep us quiet.

Cultural influences

In September 2006, the world was saddened by the death of a man whose life had sometimes been criticized and ridiculed in his home country of Australia – "The Crocodile Hunter", Steve Irwin. Irwin was a passionate naturalist and advocate for wildlife. He made his fame on the US Discovery network, watched by at least 200 million people, he played the role of the ocker Aussie who was fearless and unstoppable. Steve used language that came naturally to him, and that foreigners wanted to hear from Aussies. In turn, his language became his signature: 'Crikey!' 'Mate!' 'Crocs Rule!'

Thank God Steve Irwin didn't give up his extraordinary life's quest when some of his countrymen shunned him because of his tactics and 'ocker act'! Thank God he persisted with his signature language that communicated his cause even as the critics sharpened their knives!

Irwin was a man who lived and spoke big. He didn't give a damn about how he looked; he powerfully used his language to recruit people to his cause and he showed Australians how they can be proud of their 'can-do' spirit and the language that is innately theirs.

When news of his death echoed around the world, I, like many others, waited to hear from his grieving wife, Terri. She chose not to speak at his funeral, seen by hundreds of millions of people around the world, but instead granted two inter-views almost a month after Steve's freak death on the Barrier Reef: one with Channel Nine Australia (which was a world exclusive) and the other with legendary broadcaster Barbara Walters from ABC America.

Terri Irwin's interview, seen by 2.5 million Australians in a TV ratings bonanza, was a wonderful example of how it is culturally and humanly acceptable to be honest and uncontrollably emotional before an audience.

American-born Terri showed us how honest and real reactions and emotions, fused with expressive, accurate and powerful language, can work. Even the network's choice of emotive music, which underscored the interview, didn't leave an uncomfortable feeling among most viewers. That's because Terri Irwin spoke and revealed the truth. And we smelled that.

I was empathetically moved by Terri when she painted a word picture about her unenviable role as a mother who had to impart the news of daddy's death while looking into the eyes of her daughter Bindi, so heartbreakingly similar to her father's. Also, when she fought back the tears to share how son Robert (Bob) told her: 'I wish I could get sick so I could go to heaven with daddy.'

Terri spluttered while absorbing the scene before her: 'I love Australia. Your thoughts and prayers are really felt. They're gonna get me through.' Most viewers didn't cringe at her declaration. Why? Because when honest emotion and touching eloquence are present, they reach out to our humanity. And we instinctively get it.

Steve Irwin in his life, and Terri Irwin in his death, have been ground-breaking in how Australians use and accept communication. They have shown how finding and using an honest, passionate and emotional voice is OK and has a place within Australia's cultural identity and communication framework.

Britain's celebrity chef Jamie Oliver uses the same sort of colloquial style and presentation as Steve Irwin did. And he's made it a part of his trademark signature and success. He's a boy from Clavering, Essex and you hear it. He is young, so he uses groovy language and even borrows from outside the English language like using the Hindi word "Pukka" when something is brilliant or cooked or ripe. He is spontaneous and unstuffy and isn't trying to be something he is not, rather he uses what he is to make cooking and eating well more accessible.

Accents

As a New Zealander, I have had the experience of not being understood when travelling overseas. According to other English speakers, we often speak too quickly, and our vocal expression is clipped and disconnected from expressive body language.

We need to be patient and listen to other cultures' ways of expressing themselves. Tune your ear to different ways of speaking. I taught movement to actors in San Antonio, Texas, and started to enunciate my vowel sounds more clearly because the actors could not understand my diction.

Be patient and really listen when people with accents are speaking. We all want to be heard. I struggled to understand a friend who was born in India when we first met, but, after time, my ear became accustomed to his accent. I needed to make more of an effort to concentrate when I first spent time with him. Encourage people for whom English is a second language to be brave and speak out, otherwise they will continue to hold back and not participate.

Power and authority

Deep voices tend to be associated with power. Men therefore have a natural advantage in sounding powerful and authoritative. Early social conditioning teaches most women to speak like little ladies. I have a number of female clients who are experts in their professional fields, but their voices let them down. Why? They are softly spoken and sound like little girls. Therefore they're not always taken seriously when they speak. Never underestimate the power of your voice.

> Volume is not to be sought in high-tension use of the voice, nor in loudness or shouting, but in raising and lowering intonations, in the gradual expansion from the piano to forte and in their mutual relationship.
> *Constantin Stanislavski*

I recall coaching a manager to sound more assertive on the phone when she was calling her boss overseas. She felt intimidated by him, so I asked her to role-play with me. What she was saying was fine, but her tone was very hesitant, apologetic and lacked conviction. After an hour of practice, she started to sound more in control and more confident.

> The right to speak is a right we all have. The vast majority of us already possess superb vocal and speech instruments which we can wield better in order to assert that right.
> *Patsy Rodenburg*

This is some of my most challenging work because it involves undoing years and years of deeply ingrained habits. Timid-sounding people often lack credibility in the eyes of their colleagues. Social conditioning and physiology influence our voices, but we can learn to use them in different ways.

Gestures

Gestures can help you to emphasize points when you speak. They can be very powerful aids, but only if they are definite and appropriate to what is being said. Repetitive gestures simply distract an audience, as do little twitchy movements of the hands. If you want to make a gesture, make it big. As a useful gauge, get as much space as possible between the upper arm and your side. People often gesture while clamping their upper arms to their sides so that the gesture is made from the elbow. This looks inhibited, tense and shy. When you've finished making a gesture, either turn it into another one or let your arm relax so that it returns back to your side.

Do you like your voice?

I don't know how many times I have heard a client say, 'I do not like my voice.' My response to that is get over it; make friends with your voice.

How would you describe your voice? What is the tone like? How would you describe the voices of your friends and colleagues?

Select a few and find an adjective to describe them, such as deep, rich, low, squeaky, sexy, passionate or authoritative.

Ask someone you trust to describe your voice. Record yourself speaking and listen to how you sound. Are you happy with your voice? Write down all the aspects that you would like to change. For example: more projection, clearer diction, more colour, more energy, a more pleasant tone, wider range of pitch or improved ability to alter pace.

I remember being told by a voice teacher in America that my voice was my weakness and would hinder my acting career. Devastated as I was to hear this, I decided to invest in my voice with regular tuition. My voice was fairly high-pitched and at times I spoke too fast. I always wanted a richer tone and a deeper voice, and eventually achieved this through many hours of practice and working with a voice technician.

Retraining your voice does take time, because you're breaking old habits and learning new ones. I remember a newsreader friend helping me to change my telephone voice-mail message over and over for half an hour until he was satisfied with the tone in the message. He said my delivery wasn't clear enough and lacked variation of pitch. Get honest feedback about your voice from people whose opinions you value. This practice enabled me to experiment with my voice and increase my self-confidence as a communicator.

Accepting your voice
Many clients tell me they don't like their voices. When I ask why, most say, 'I don't like my accent' or 'I've been told my voice is too quiet' and so on. There is nothing fundamentally wrong with your voice. It's an important part of who you are. However, there are skills you can learn to improve the voice you've been born with and sound more professional and convincing.

Delivery is the secret of public speaking.
Demosthenes

As children we love to imitate, and usually sound like our family members. I once coached a family member for an overseas leadership position, particularly working on the speed of his delivery. He spoke so quickly during a rehearsal that I was nervous about the outcome. I concentrated on getting him to slow down his pace and eventually, with practice, he could be heard clearly. He'd never had feedback about his presentation style before. He gave an outstanding presentation and got the job of his dreams. Speaking too fast can be a sign of nervousness, and means we forget to enunciate clearly. It's fine to imitate someone else's voice when experimenting but it's more important to work on the strengths and limitations of your own voice. Learn to accept your voice, but seek feedback from experts whose ears are trained to help you sound more persuasive.

Voice production
Body alignment
Good body alignment is essential for a good voice. It is amazing how something like your balance and your posture can affect the sound of your voice. Check that you're not locking your knees and that your spine is lengthened. People, particularly women, often sit down into their pelvises, which doesn't allow the spine to lengthen. Check that your shoulders are relaxed – a dead give-away that speakers are nervous is when their shoulders are up around their ears. Check also that your head is balanced on the top of your spine. You will feel that the back of your neck is long and your face will be parallel with whatever wall you're facing. This simply means that you're not jutting your chin forward or tucking it down and looking at your audience from under your eyebrows, the way the very shy young Princess Diana used to do. Check for tension around the mouth and particularly the jaw – jaw tension is extremely common and affects both clarity and tone.

Exercise
Imagine a piece of string running through your head, down the back of your neck and spine. Now imagine it lifting you up through the top of your head, causing your spine to straighten. Ensure your weight is evenly spread over both sides of your

body. Turn your head gently to the right, then return to centre, then left, then return to centre. Repeat ten times.

Breathing

We are notoriously lazy about our intake of breath and it is very common to find people constantly allowing air into only the top part of their lungs. This means the voice lacks depth and often sounds tense.

Exercise

Practise breathing through the nose not the mouth. Close your mouth and take three deep breaths to the bottom of your lungs. However, when we speak we take air in through the mouth (it would take us forever, otherwise). Huff all your breath out, without collapsing the body, and what is called the elastic recoil of breath will take place. You can aid this by releasing your belly, as though everything from your waist drops down to the pelvic floor, the instant you know the breath is going to come in your body.

Diction

Articulating correctly means pronouncing your vowels and consonants. There's not much point in giving a brilliant speech if you can't be understood. The English language contains different lengths of vowel sounds. For example, it will take you slightly longer to say the diphthong 'I' than it does to say the short 'i' in 'it'. Check that you don't reduce all vowels to short vowels. Consonants must be used firmly. If you have to say a word like 'ghosts', you must work your way right through the 's', then 't', then 's' because anything else will be unclear to your listeners. They will spend precious seconds trying to sort out by context what you've said and therefore miss your next point.

Exercise

Tape yourself and listen to your voice. Practise tongue twisters or repetition phrases, such as 'Unique New York, unique New York' or 'Red leather yellow leather, red leather yellow leather'.

Intonation

Variation of pitch adds life and colour to your voice. Think in terms of highs and lows or allowing the voice to rise and fall naturally. It doesn't take very much alteration of pitch to make your voice interesting. Usually, you alter pitch for emphasis and you should do this on only the main syllable of a word. For example, with 'Oh, that's interesting', you could pitch up on the 'in' of interesting. Or you could pitch up on 'that's' and you would get a slightly different meaning. Try it!

Exercise

Read stories to children (or to anyone who is kind enough to listen to you). Experiment with highs and lows, injecting passion into your voice.

Sing the 'doh ray me' scales.

Inflections

In some parts of the world, people raise the pitch of their voice at the end of a sentence, thereby turning it into a question. This can be confusing for the listener. Often, this rising inflection can be attributed to a soft palate (located at the back of the roof of the mouth) which is lowering instead of lifting. It is very difficult both to articulate and to use wide pitch range when the soft palate is lowered.

Exercise

Get into the habit of making statements. Think 'down' at the ends of sentences, and don't turn the sentence into a question. Get feedback as to whether or not you do this.

Avoiding falsetto pitch

Many women speak in a pitch which is unnaturally high. They are often using 'falsetto quality' instead of 'speech quality'. In speech quality the vocal folds are short and thick, producing a different tone quality from falsetto, where the vocal folds are thin and stiff. Try to achieve glottal onset of tone, which means the vocal folds come together the instant before speech starts – try using the cheeky 'uh oh' sounds we make when we see trouble looming. This usually places us in speech quality.

A characteristic of falsetto quality is that the breath escapes just before the tone starts, and using the vowel sounds in the exercises below will also ensure that this doesn't happen.

Exercise

A good way to avoid falsetto voice pitch is to practise lots of sentences where each word begins with a vowel. 'Angry ants activate acid' or 'Elegant elephants eat everything' are good examples.

Sometimes, too, it is useful simply to count backwards from five, lowering the pitch slightly each time. By the time you get to 'two' or 'one', you've probably hit the pitch which is more naturally your own, instead of the one you habitually use.

Rhythm

If you want to turn your audience off and send them to sleep, speak in a monotone. If you're bored, you'll be more likely to speak in a monotone, so inject some enthusiasm into your voice.

Exercise
Practise singing a song that has rhythm or reading a poem out loud.

Volume
Your volume depends on the size of the room. If you are speaking in a small room, use your natural voice. If in a larger room, project to the last row. If you can't be heard, all your key messages are lost. Never push from the larynx to get louder. Rather, use the muscles of the back to ensure that you achieve more volume, by trying the exercise below.

Exercise
Imagine you have a balloon under each armpit and that you are squashing them against your sides as you speak without the audience seeing any effort on your part. This engages the latissimus dorsi muscles. Next, find what movement creates a 'fat waist', where your waist muscles on either side seem to push out a little. It's what happens naturally when you actively hold your breath. A little engagement of these muscles (the quadratus lamborum muscles on either side of the spine) will increase your volume by 10–15 decibels without putting stress on your larynx.

Get someone to stand at the back of the room when you are rehearsing your speech and tell you if you are sufficiently projecting your voice.

Pace
Speed means the number of words spoken per minute. Most of us speak at a rate of about 160–200 words per minute. In December 1961, John F Kennedy gave a speech at the rate of 327 words per minute – I hope the audience could understand it!

Move quickly through the unimportant words and phrases and slow down the important ones. It is this variety of pace which makes us sound interesting. A constant pace, either fast or slow, is difficult to stay tuned in to – it becomes mesmeric.

Exercise
Listen to other speakers and become conscious of their pace. When do they speed up? When do they slow down? Listening to others will improve your skill.

Pauses

Actors use a pause to create suspense and gain the audience's attention. Pausing is more effective than using fillers like 'um' and 'ah'. Silence is powerful. Listeners tend to hang on in anticipation of a speaker choosing exactly the word they need to describe something accurately. Never forget that we are fascinated by the spectacle of someone in the act of thinking.

Exercise
Pause and inhale every time you go to say 'um' or 'ah' or use a filler word. Ask friends and colleagues if you use 'ums' and 'ahs' in your conversations. Film yourself giving a two-minute speech, and work towards not saying 'um' any more than once a minute.

Build to a pause by making three specific points, each one slightly higher in pitch than the one before. By the time you've done that, you've earned yourself a pause, while the listeners digest the information you've given them and you let the words 'hang in the air' for a short space of time. The three-point plan seems to be particularly satisfying for human beings to listen and relate to. You can often 'cap' these points with a summing-up sentence in a lower pitch.

Overcoming stuttering

It takes patience, skill and professional support to overcome a stutter. Former Prime Minister Winston Churchill had a stutter when he started his career. Through sheer determination and effort he became one of the most accomplished orators in the twentieth century.

I have worked with a number of clients who stutter when they are nervous, especially when having to speak on television, including a chief executive who was terrified he would stutter if stuck for words. The more he relaxed his voice and practised vocal warm-up exercises like humming and relaxing the body, the less he would stutter.

Another businessman came for coaching after a stuttering episode on national television. I felt so sorry for him when I saw the footage and his level of discomfort. It was a news item and he panicked when confronted with a challenging question. He stuttered over and over. Fear does extraordinary things to the body and voice.

If you are a chronic stutterer, you may need to hire a voice coach or go to regular classes to overcome your fears. There is often an emotional or psychological issue behind the stutter.

Exercise
Try allowing an easy, full breath in and chant what you want to say. Chanting requires an even flow of breath and means that you must work at a slowish pace in order to articulate all the sounds in the words. From there, it is relatively easy to release the chant (which is halfway between speech and singing) back to ordinary speech.

Microphones

Practise and make sure you feel comfortable with a microphone. I've seen many speakers turn up to speak who have never used one before. Microphones enable you to speak more easily in a large room. They were designed so you could be heard and not strain your voice.

Make sure you turn your microphone off when you are no longer presenting lest you do the same as a television newsreader who forgot to turn her microphone off when going to the bathroom. An embarrassing mistake! I also have had several embarrassing experiences when forgetting to turn my microphone off. I recall a training session when I tried to surprise my co-facilitator with a birthday cake. I still had my lapel microphone on when I spoke to the hotel caterer, saying, 'It's going to take her by surprise.' She heard me and so did the team of young legal administrators we were training.

Chapter 12 on technology has a list of tips for using your microphone effectively.

Exercise
Do a sound check at least one hour prior to your presentation. If you've never used a microphone before, practise with it so it's not foreign to you. Never get up on a platform or rostrum and say, 'Is this microphone on? Can you hear me?' You will look unprepared and it's a flat way to open your speech.

If you want to practise at home with a microphone, many sound systems have a karaoke function which allows you to practise listening to yourself speak.

Looking after your voice
Taking care of your voice is really important. Linda Cartwright teaches her students how to look after their vocal folds (also known as vocal cords) in the larynx. The diagram overleaf shows a view of the larynx – note the false folds situated just above the vocal folds. The false folds are two masses which come together to close up the airspace above

LARYNX

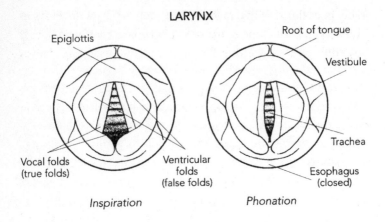

Epiglottis

Root of tongue

Vestibule

Trachea

Vocal folds
(true folds)

Ventricular
folds
(false folds)

Esophagus
(closed)

Inspiration   *Phonation*

the true vocal folds, which upsets vibration and the sound quality of your voice.

Laughing relaxes the vocal cords by allowing the true folds to vibrate without hindrance, which is what happens when a speaker 'opens the throat'. Ellen Sarewitz said: 'When I become tense and the sound is strained, my singing teacher makes me laugh, which immediately removes the stress and allows the notes to go into the right place.'

Many auctioneers strain their voices and develop nodules on their vocal folds, because they do not retract their false folds before speaking. I spent five years training auctioneers and was horrified to hear that some of them had a nip of whisky before running an auction. They seemed to think it would clear their throats. The auctioneers who retracted their false folds, anchored the larynx with muscles in the back and used some 'twang quality' in their voices, said that they didn't strain their voices.

Carla Franks said: 'I used to make a warm lemon and honey drink for Elton John backstage after doing his make-up. A lot of singers use this simple remedy to soothe the throat.' On many occasions, I have made a steam inhalation with Vicks or Tiger Balm®. Of course, the best advice is to rest the voice. If you think you are getting laryngitis, just stop talking. Never strain your voice.

University of Sydney researcher Kate Madill told the National Conference of Speech Pathology in Australia that demand for therapy to speak more effectively and to prevent voice injury was at an all-time high. This demand is largely driven by the rise of call centres and other service industries, where a growing proportion of people speak for a living. Madill said that if people were shown a better way of speaking, they could consciously choose to use it and, over time, their body would naturally default to the new way.

Warming up your voice
Actor Theresa Healey has her own particular warm-up routine. She says that every night, before she participates in a debate or gives a speech, she opens her mouth wide and goes 'Blaaaaaa-aaaaaaaah!' at full volume. Stress, stage fright, tiredness and emotional trauma all have a negative effect on your voice. Never go out to speak without warming up your voice first. Chapter 8 has a full warm-up programme.

TIPS ON A BETTER VOICE (by Linda Cartwright)

Stand easily and well, with the body in alignment.

Practise relaxing the body (and that doesn't mean collapsing it) while sharply focusing the mind.

Don't slide into a sentence so that your full voice is achieved only on the third to fifth word. Start the first word meaning business.

Make the very little effort needed to retract the false folds if you are needing to project your voice.

Sharpen up your diction – take the time to utilize consonants. Consonants are heard less easily than vowels, so, in order to be heard, bring your consonants up to the level of your vowels.

Flow phrases on, so that you are shaping the words into a form that is easily understood by your listeners. We hear in phrases, not in a series of individual words. Often, in order to try to achieve clarity, people will speak giving each word the same value. This will simply sound pedantic and monotonous.

Variety is the spice of life. Vary pitch and pace, according to thought patterns. We often interrupt ourselves, remember an example, or bring in a new idea when we're speaking. Each time we do this, we bring a renewed energy to our voices. We speak a little faster, and we slightly alter our pitch. Check that you're doing this, even if you know your speech by heart. It will give the appearance of spontaneity and keep the listeners' attention.

Practise supporting the larynx by anchoring with the latissimus dorsi (the muscles under your shoulder blades) and the quadratus lumborum muscles (in your lower back).

Make eye contact with your audience. This will provide focus for your voice and help you to make your audience listen. People often don't listen unless the speaker makes them do so.

5

FIRST IMPRESSIONS

You don't get a second chance to make a good first impression.
John Malloy

Do first impressions really matter? A person makes a judgement about you within ten seconds of meeting you. Good first
impressions can make you new friends, build your business
and your networks, improve your personal and business
relationships, make you money and even influence how you
feel about a place or environment. Think London cabbies.
Whenever I arrive back in the UK after a stint abroad, if my
black cab driver says, 'Allo love', and is a joy to share the car
with, being back in London becomes a moment of joy. Bad
first impressions can ruin your professional reputation for
years, lose you a second interview, and put people off working
or socializing with you. A sour-faced cabbie can ruin your
arrival or homecoming. He can forget about a tip!

A friend who is a top business-communications trainer in
the UK met me for the first time in the late eighties when I
was director of the Performing Arts School. Months after our
meeting, he told me he thought I was arrogant when we were

introduced. I was shocked, but when I honestly thought about it, I recall being busy at the time and not really giving him the time of day. Subsequently we ended up being friends as his background was also theatre and our career paths were similar. That feedback made me realize how powerful first impressions are; I didn't come across as a warm person, which is not the usual me. My impression wasn't good for my personal brand or for the organization I was running at the time.

Think back to feedback you may have received. Take it seriously. Be aware of your body language and be more conscious of people watching and observing.

What first impression do you make?

Ask three people in business whom you respect what their first impressions were of you when you met them. Call them on the phone or go and see them and record their answers. If it's all favourable, keep on asking until you get some constructive negative criticism. Ask them to be specific – for example, if you came across as cold, arrogant or cynical, was it in your eyes, body language or in the tone of your voice? Keep on asking and listen without defending yourself. Write it down and remember the answers. Do something positive with the information. Don't beat yourself up or judge yourself, but move forward with your new information.

A businesswoman I respect, who is a Head of Finance for a communications company, told me she often experiences me as a whirlwind of energy. A part of me liked this feedback, but another part didn't because it could mean I am there and then gone with no time to connect.

I'll keep asking for feedback because this helps me to improve the way I come across to my audience. Asking for feedback helps you to be confident that people perceive you as you would like them to – as the genuine, authentic person you are.

Ellen is a company director. Her team was pitching for a large piece of business presenting to a significant audience in a public relations company in London. Ellen arrived on time with two of her colleagues. The group managing director of her company misjudged the time, arriving one hour late. He spent ten minutes apologizing, and at that moment Ellen knew that they had lost the pitch before even starting. 'I was furious and very disappointed because we should have won it,' she said.

Always focus on the end goal. Arrive early and always leave more time. Assume nothing.

This bad error of judgement lost the job. If you are late for a pitch you are sending out a message to the client that says: 'You don't matter and I don't care.' To create good first impressions you need to respect everyone and make sure that nothing like this ever happens. The group MD didn't just let down the client, he also let down his team and the reputation of the organization. First impressions always count.

I was late for a business meeting with a new client, a profes-sional services company, and arrived with my colleague, takeaway coffee in hand, five minutes after the agreed time. Years later the HR manager told her client that she had not been impressed with me. I was defensive and embarrassed about my unprofessional behaviour. I was not committed enough and did not get the new business I went there for. I have never forgotten it.

Also, make sure you are really familiar with the names of your clients and business collaborators to avoid gaffes like this one of mine with a Dutch man.

'Hi Dork, how are you?' I smiled with my hand out-stretched.

Senior businessman, DIRK, flatly responded, 'Well I've been called worse.'

The General Manager of the company I had been hired to consult with, of which Dirk was an employee, looked at me with disgust.

My company awarded me the yearly prize for biggest stuff up.

Giving honest feedback

After a presentation, always ask for a debrief from a colleague you trust. I've worked with Allie Webber, a talented writer and media trainer, for many years. We co-facilitated workshops and seminars together, debriefing after every training day and critiquing each other's performances. Our business and personal relationship has grown through constructive criticism.

Don't be scared to ask 'How do I come across? What can I do to improve?' You won't necessarily want to hear the answers and responses and you don't have to believe or accept what you hear. Many clients tell me they're hungry for feedback; this means they simply don't ask for it enough. Don't wait to be told by your employer at your performance review. We need to know so we can improve our interpersonal skills and show the real us when speaking in public. Remember, you won't always like what you hear, and you don't have to agree with it completely, but at least have a think about whether there is a kernel of truth in the feedback you receive.

Ask for feedback

Some questions you might ask the person giving feedback to consider include:

- Did the audience/client warm to me?
- Do they like and trust me?
- Do they respect and admire my approach and manner?
- Am I relaxing to be around?
- Do I look professional?
- What are my strengths and weaknesses?
- What can I do better next time?

Many of my clients seek help when they have an important job interview. That first impression may or may not get them the second interview. I admire clients who ask how they come across. 'How did you find my manner in my first session with you?' 'Do I have any presence?' 'Can you give me feedback as to how you find me?' 'What is missing and what do I need to do to improve?'

Giving honest feedback in a caring way is an important skill. If you are asked to give feedback, the main points to remember are:

- Use 'I' statements, not 'you' statements. 'I' implies that the feedback giver is taking responsibility for the feedback; 'you' implies blame.
- Be very specific so the person receiving the feedback knows exactly what you're talking about. For example, 'I notice you played with your tie during the presentation. I thought you looked nervous,' is better than 'You looked nervous during the presentation.'
- Follow the Commend – Recommend – Commend pattern, by providing positive feedback, followed by constructive negative feedback, and finishing with positive feedback. For example, 'I liked your succinct snappy phrases. I would feel more relaxed if you smiled. You have such a genuine smile.'

Trust

The audience decides whether or not to trust you based on their first impressions. When we meet someone for the first time, we always think: Do I trust you? Do I want to be with you? Do I like you? Do I want to work with you? Do I want to listen and invest time and energy here? What's in it for me to be in a relationship with you? First impressions are of critical importance in public speaking because your audience will subconsciously decide whether or not to listen to your message depending on the type of impression you make.

Cultural sensitivity

Making an effort with greetings in the language of your audience is worth it in my opinion. The audience or client respect you more, so your confidence increases. It does not matter if your pronunciation is incorrect and gets a smile. People feel acknowledged and at home. It builds rapport and shows you care. Any sign, either through language or gesture from you, that underscores you are sensitive to another country's language and culture is a sure way to enhance communication.

Make the impression you want to make

How do you do this? Tom is a senior partner in a professional-services company. He asked me to give him a formula for networking while we were discussing his billings and his new business for the month. He wanted to make more of an impact with potential clients and leave a more lasting impression with people in business. Here is what I suggested:

The Ten P Formula

1. Planning what you say and do

Making an impression requires making an effort. Plan your

wardrobe, your key messages and your conversation starters. Define your objective and goal – is it to bring in more business? How will you do this? For example, you could plan three new meetings a month with three chief executives or prospective clients.

2. Preparation of materials, grooming and environment
Invest in your image. For example, buy new clothing and insist on plants and flowers in the room where you're speaking. Dress your set and think of the room as your stage. Your environment can help you to look good.

3. Packaging yourself and your speech
You are a bundle of key messages so wrap them up well. For example, you could theme your speech around your personal and business values, or reinvent yourself by changing your wardrobe, hair and accessories. Brainstorm with marketing experts so they get to understand what is inside the parcel – you. Who are you?

4. Pace yourself, your energy levels, body and voice
Work with a voice coach and practise breathing exercises to calm yourself so you are aware of slowing down and more conscious of not speeding up your dialogue. Learn about your voice so you can have shades, light and colour in your speech. Pacing your speech and pausing effectively make you more credible.

5. Paint a positive picture of yourself and others
Use stories to engage people. Talk in pictures. Produce a business card that paints a picture of you so it attracts business and reflects your brand truthfully. Do the colours agree with your business values? Would it end up in the bin or make such

an impression the client wants to keep it? Are you someone people will find it exciting to listen to? Remember always to speak positively about yourself, your colleagues and your organization during a presentation.

6. PR – give yourself a good name

Hire a public-relations company or consultant to make you look good, or read books on PR and learn the ropes. Marketing is essential when wanting to make a strong impression. Don't let yourself down by giving yourself bad press.

7. Pamper yourself before your speech so your audience can appreciate you

Have regular massages, get your hair done on the day of the speech or interview. Feeling good often means looking good. Prioritize time for yourself. Pampering yourself is a sign of self-respect.

8. Panache – adopt a confident style and manner

Dare to be a little more flamboyant. Go outside your comfort zone and enrol in an acting class. Consider hiring an image consultant. Observe how people you admire dress and act when presenting.

9. Passion

Show others you're willing to share your feelings and opinions with emotion, moving them so much they are inspired to listen and want more. It's perfectly OK to show you care by wearing your heart on your sleeve.

10. Participate

Share yourself more with people, and your audience will feel included. Try to make all your communication interactive –

people pay more attention when they feel included. Communication is a two-way exchange.

Your friends made an impression on you

Blessed with a close group of friends, I often think of the first time I met them individually. These people, whom I love and confide in, have made a huge impact on my life. With each and every one of them I can remember the first moment I met them. Take your mind back to the times you met your close friends and clients. Why were you drawn to them? Was it their appearance, energy, cheekiness, personality, intelligence, spark, beauty, dignity? These people were all strangers at one time, but through conversations, dinners, exchanges of ideas and information, they have become friends. Every one of them made a first impression that stayed with you.

What does it mean to you when someone makes an impression? What do you look for? What do you expect? What turns you off? What draws you in? Every day I meet someone new in business, a new client to build a long-term or short-term relationship with depending on the situation. Every day I form an impression of them as they do of me.

When did you last make a good impression that changed your life forever? When did you last form an impression about a client that resulted in a friendship? When did a stranger give you praise about the conversation or encounter you had with that person?

Brag more

I think antipodeans and the British don't brag enough. In my opinion we hold back about our achievements. I loved being a part of the American culture during my time living in the US because it was acceptable to talk proudly about your skills. Don't be afraid to brag, but do it with sincerity and integrity.

I'm often amazed when working with clients to discover they hold back about some of their major achievements. Share who you really are at an interview; the interviewee wants to meet the real you. Communicate from your heart.

Body language

Body language is such an important component of first impressions. Think about the difference between a speaker standing upright with shoulders back and head held high, and a slouching person reading from notes and not making eye contact with the audience. The words spoken could be exactly the same, but the impression on the audience is very different. Become more aware of your posture and notice any distracting habits that need to go. Also keep in mind that sometimes your body becomes your language, and your gestures and movements become the words.

Those of us who travel know this well as we make ourselves understood in non-English-speaking countries through using mime and gesture, rather than the spoken word. This is also the case with those who are hearing-impaired or who have certain disabilities. The lesson here is be aware of the power of your body to communicate and be ready to use it instead of words when the moment arises.

Read Chapter 3 on body language for a thorough discussion on this topic.

Your working environment

Do the fresh flowers on your desk send out a positive message? Does that rotten banana sitting next to your computer or apple core in your car send out a positive message?

Project the image you want others to have of you. If you want to be perceived as disorganized and inefficient then continue to have a messy desk. If you want to be perceived as professional then make an effort to clear your desk regularly. Does your desk reflect your personality? I learn a lot about people when I walk into their office. Don't be afraid to show a little of your personality on your noticeboard. Personal photos are a handy icebreaker.

Most companies have a policy about office tidiness. If clients, visitors and potential clients walk around and visit in your work area then it's important to think about how you want to be perceived. I used to be a little too relaxed about my work area but have got my act together and made an effort, realizing that people judge and notice detail. Don't let all the hard work that has gone into a presentation to a client be undone by the unspoken messages of disorganization and clutter from your work environment.

CVs

First impressions on paper matter too. What does it say about you or your brand if you have spelling mistakes in your CV? It says you are lazy and lack attention to detail and the client receiving the document is not worthy of respect.

I have invested time, effort and money into presenting my résumés over the years, updating them regularly and paying a skilled writer to check the contents. Get it right from the beginning so it is easy to update when you need to. I'm sent curricula vitae frequently from trainers looking for work or PR graduates wanting contacts. The ones that make a good impression are noticed and acted upon. How you present yourself on paper is as important as how you present yourself in person, especially when making contact for the first time.

Achieving the right tone in your CV is important – try to find the middle ground between over and underselling. Clean, crisp, matter-of-fact CVs that give a hint of personality will be noticed. Your CV should reflect your brand – are you witty and warm? Cool, calm and collected? Intelligent and enquiring? You must present yourself consistently with your CV – if you say you have great attention to detail, don't arrive at the interview with scuffed shoes.

Get hold of three excellent curricula vitae so you have a comparison or benchmark. Work on yours then show it to friends and ask for feedback – they will notice things which passed you by. Would you hire yourself based on your CV?

Other written communication

For many people, email is an important communication tool. However, we often present ourselves poorly via this medium. An email reflects your personality, your company brand and your attitude. Take more time thinking about how you want to be perceived before you press the send button. Spell check and proofread your message carefully. Many people have had a disastrous situation because they have not paid attention to whom they were addressing their email.

Have you ever handed out or received dog-eared business cards? All stationery, especially business cards, is part of your overall image. Taking a credentials document to a meeting after you have spilt coffee on it or accidentally wiped lipstick on it will hinder your efforts to make a good first impression.

Job interviews

I have always paid attention to feedback, and often directly ask for it. Not knowing what impression you've made can leave you wondering. I remember pitching for a training account back in the early 1990s. I badly wanted this account and gave it everything I had. I'd done my research and was very organized and prepared. I believed I could make a differ-ence to this company and told them so with conviction! I had spent hours getting my clothing just right and hired a makeup artist. I was invited back for a second interview.

However, after the second interview, I was convinced I had blown it and was very depressed when I walked out of the high-rise building. The manager who interviewed me gave nothing away. To my surprise I won the account up against many trainers who were more experienced. To this day I will never be really sure what it was that got me the work but I know I must have made a good impression because I was awarded the contract. So, never make an assumption about first impressions – you cannot mind-read and you may have made a favourable impression when you think you haven't.

> Learn to get in touch with the innermost essence of your being. This essence is beyond ego.
> *Deepak Chopra*

Thirty per cent of my work is about helping clients prepare for and win the job of their dreams. Their success is my success.

My great friend and work collaborator Penelope Barr, who is a marketing and communications professional in the UK, gives excellent advice on how to leave an impression when you are being interviewed for a job. This is her checklist that can become yours as well:

1. Do your research. If you are serious about the role, do your homework – which doesn't mean a quick glance at the company website before the interview. Know what is happening in the industry and how your target company fits into it. Know what they are famous for, who their

clients are, what their culture is like and the type of people they employ.

2. Know your interviewer. If possible, try and get a thumbnail description of the person who is interviewing you so you can tailor your responses to capture her interest to best effect. For example, a 'detail' person will want to know more of the 'nitty gritty' about your work and the results you have achieved.

3. Be prepared from the outset. The first interview is often pitched as 'seeing whether there is the right chemistry', but don't be lulled into thinking that you won't be asked some hard questions. Know what you want to say and how you want to present yourself from the outset. Be able to validate your claims, so have work samples. Also, think of the toughest question they could ask you and prepare a response.

4. Know your strengths and weaknesses. Be able to describe clearly, and in a few punchy points, how your unique work and personal skills and attributes can add value. Be careful that your one weakness is not inferred to be greater than it is. For example, 'I work too hard' could be misconstrued to mean 'I don't like hard work'!

5. Be conservative. Less is definitely more when it comes to how you dress. Keep it simple, clean and uncluttered. You want the focus to be on you, not your earrings or necktie.

6. Know where you are going and leave plenty of time. There is usually a window of 'forgiveness' about being late, but it can still send the wrong message, especially at the first interview. It doesn't help your stress levels either!

7. Ask questions. You are not only the interviewee but an interviewer as well, so think carefully about the things you want to know about the role and the company and ask them.

8. Be polite. Show respect.
9. Read between the lines. Often you will never know what a person really thinks of you, but still ask for feedback if you haven't gone to the next stage in the process or been offered the role.
10. Never give up. Pursue your dream, despite a few knock-backs. Don't take rejection personally – there are often a lot of people vying for the same jobs, so learn from the experience and polish your performance for next time. In a market of this size you need to be truly outstanding.
11. Finally, always be true to yourself.

Networking

Networking is an essential business tool and being confident allows you to make a vibrant first impression. Networking with confidence will help your career and help you to grow as a person. Doing business is all about making excellent first impressions, and this can depend on your ability to communicate with strangers.

Making small talk at functions is a frightening experience for many people. Clients often ask me to teach them how to practise the art of chitchat at a business cocktail party. How do you get past 'hello'? My advice is to present yourself passionately and always show the real you. People buy from the heart and respond to sincerity. Every time you meet someone for the first time, focus on that person's needs. Take the focus off you by thinking about the other person. Be truthful, be spontaneous, be professional, be authentic and bring some fun into that person's life while she is talking with you.

An induction programme I designed for graduates in a global chartered accountancy firm used romance as a metaphor. The participants had to think about what they do at a party when they are attracted to someone and want to make a good impression.

What do they do and say on a date when they are trying to come across as interesting? It was one of my favourite seminars because the answers were always applicable to business. The most common answer was 'I listen carefully.'

One tricky brief I had was to design a schmoozing workshop for a law firm. It took me a while to get my head around the objective; schmoozing is a delicious word but what does it really mean in a business context? It's all about making contacts and building rapport, and is an essential tool for success. To build warm relationships in business you need to have good social skills. Think of everyone you meet as a potential good friend or potential business contact.

Listening

The golden rule here is to avoid talking about yourself all the time. I see many people asking questions at business and private functions but not listening to the answers. It seems they only want to hear the sound of their own voice! When I first worked for a training company called ETC (Experiential Training Company) in the early nineties, I used to attend meetings with the company director, Trevor Lawrence. I would observe him listening to his clients more then talking. He was an expert at this and it soon became obvious why he won repeat business. His clients trusted him. They felt he listened to their problems and then created a positive solution for them.

Your appearance

We may wish it didn't matter, but it does. How we present ourselves physically makes a big contribution to successful first impressions. Clothing really does matter when you are giving a speech, pitching for new business or meeting a client for the first time, as your audience will be looking for nonverbal messages as to whether you and your message can be trusted. Spend some time reading Chapter 15 on image and grooming for tips on brushing up your wardrobe and presenting yourself well.

TIPS ON MAKING A GOOD FIRST IMPRESSION

Plan your wardrobe well in advance of an important speech, interview or meeting. Wear clothing that makes you stand tall and feel proud. Avoid seductive clothing as it will send out inappropriate signals, and now is not the time to break in new shoes!

Check your personal hygiene: bad breath, body odour and unshaven faces all send a strong message of not caring about yourself.

Take pride in your appearance – a good haircut and a manicure speak volumes.

Watch out for overpowering perfume or cologne, and if applicable, don't overdo the makeup – it can be very distracting.

Practise your handshake – a bonecruncher or a limp fish is off-putting. Carrying a briefcase in your left hand allows you to shake hands with your right. Avoid carrying both a briefcase and a handbag – you don't have three hands!

Smile and radiate warmth when you meet people for the first time, and look them in the eye.

Appear alert and energetic, even if you are exhausted.

Ask questions and be interested when hearing the answer. People love to be listened to. Practise being a good listener.

Your first impressions are within your control. Don't ever underestimate their importance.

6

WRITING THE WORDS

Great leaders from the past have not necessarily been great speakers, but the thoughts that they have fired from their bows penetrate our hearts to this day.
Vijay Eswaran

To make a speech, you must have something to say. If you have nothing to say on a topic, you have no reason to give a speech about it.

Every time I am asked to speak to an audience I sit down and ask myself one question before I write: What is it that I really want to say? What do I want my speech to accomplish? I often spend a couple of hours – sometimes longer – thinking about the words and my subject matter and organizing it in my mind before putting it on paper.

Don't wing it!

Give me one good reason why you would want to speak in public without adequate preparation. Is it procrastination? Lack of time? You like the pressure? Even if you write three key messages or bullet points down on a scrap of paper, it's better than nothing. It's a fallacy that experienced communicators don't need to prepare; the most polished and confident communicators appear that way as a result of their excellent preparation. Even when I am asked to give a short speech I find time to write my thoughts down and make sure I have noted what I really want to say.

So often my clients say to me 'I wing it' or 'I've winged it for years'. Respect your audience more, they deserve your best performance. My philosophy is: only say yes if you are willing to put in the spadework and do some preparation, otherwise you let yourself and your audience down. Put a stop to 'putting it off'.

Past beliefs about writing

Many of my clients have been told they can't write. We often believe what we are told. Was your writing praised when you were at school?

My father was the first person to believe in my writing. I remember him telling me when I was at secondary school that I wrote well. I was surprised at the time as writing was never a passion. Yet I wrote letters, poetry, journals and diaries for most of my childhood and early adulthood. I realize now that this writing discipline helped me in later years to shape my presentations.

Think of yourself as a gifted communicator on paper and write as you speak. Just get the words down and edit and cull later. I have been writing articles for business publications for a number of years now and can say that it is only by 'doing it' that you gain the confidence in yourself as a writer.

Don't let yourself feel inadequate about your writing skills – all writers learn their craft through practice and perseverance. I spent years feeling inadequate about writing speeches and media releases because I didn't train as a journalist and was surrounded by competent writers in the public-relations industry. My work and social life over the years have brought me in contact with many experienced writers: authors, press secretaries, academics, broadcasters, scriptwriters, not to mention a large number of excellent journalists – all with a craft I admired.

My feelings of inadequacy started to change when I asked for feedback from these experienced writers and continued to practise my writing. If you want to improve your writing skills, surround yourself with competent writers and ask for honest feedback. There are also many excellent writing courses available which will give you the opportunity to develop this skill.

Procrastination

A frustrating part of my job is arriving to work with clients when they have not written their speeches and have not prepared the content they are paying me to critique. The thing we all have in common as human beings is that we procrastinate. Consistently there is one question I ask the clients at the end of delivering a speech/presentation. This is: 'How long did it take you to prepare that?' I am often faced with a pause and then often hear the answer: 'Thirty minutes on the plane, before bed last night or in the morning tea break.' My response is 'not good enough'.

Writing has never been my passion or my strength; in fact I have really had to find the necessary discipline at times. It isn't exciting for me to sit and write; my passion is performing and delivering the words. Stick with it; writing is a creative process which comes from within. There are many ways to get started and to enjoy writing.

I have found a good way to get started is to have a plan. Work out exactly when and how you are going to write the content. Commit on paper or on your computer so you know what your schedule is. Even better, show someone your plan and ask them to help you stick to it by showing them your draft speech by an agreed date.

Ask yourself whether there is a valid reason for your procrastination. In the past, I've sometimes said yes to writing a speech because the financial deal was attractive or the kudos attached was appealing and every time I regretted getting involved. Think about whether you are the right person to speak. Are you qualified? Are you excited about the brief? Are you enthusiastic about writing the words? These days, if I think I'm not the best person to deliver the message, I call my agent and make a suggestion for an alternative speaker. Turning away business isn't easy, but you can get caught out if you're not an expert in the field or if you're not passionate about the subject.

Of course, the best way to avoid procrastination is to believe in yourself, find a positive attitude and just get going and write!

Find a writing process that works for you

Some of my best thinking about the structure of a speech occurs while walking at the weekends. Then I put my thoughts and ideas down on paper. I can take months if I have time on my side thinking about the key messages of a speech and being very clear in my own mind about what it is I intend to say. I then run it by someone I trust to get some feedback.

I started to write this book in shorthand on paper, which felt more creative. I dictated a few chapters to friends who typed frantically while I punched the air and walked the length of my apartment or theirs. This also felt creative and it was fun. I talked into a microphone for a while. This didn't work for me but does for many writers who then have their words transcribed. Most of my more creative ideas flowed in a café on the way to work. Many scraps of paper ended up in my bag along with paper napkins and scribbled-on newspapers.

Collaborative writing stimulates me when I'm writing a business presentation. It helps me to engage my brain. There's a great concept called peer review, which is part of my everyday business week, where I have a colleague read and revise my writing. Another set of eyes ensures that what you've written is understandable, credible and persuasive. It doesn't matter how you write as long as you do it.

Getting started

Preparation

The main key to writing a stunning speech is preparation. If you give yourself enough time to prepare properly without pressure, you'll be able to sort out any glitches and make sure you're saying what you really want to say.

How long should it take to write a speech? Your knowledge and passion for the subject will determine the appropriate preparation time. If it's a business pitch you'll spend longer because there is something at stake. How hungry are you to pull in this account? Sometimes I have spent months writing a speech. At the other end of the scale, I have also scribbled a few bullet points on the back of an envelope during a plane trip if it was for a short five-minute speech. But even in the latter example, I would still have thought about the speech for a number of hours.

What's the brief?

Listen to the brief for your speech very carefully and ask lots of questions. Write everything down. I rely on the brief and make sure I understand what my client's business is about. Try to understand the audience and the reason for the presentation before starting to write. I see many people in business underestimating the importance of the brief, and I think business is often lost as a result. We often don't listen to the client's language carefully enough.

I recall a client who wanted to learn how to deliver some bad news to her staff, but wanted to motivate them as well. She wanted to deliver the message with humour, so that people could laugh at themselves but also remember the serious intent behind the presentation. I decided to use professional actors who were skilled at improvisation to deliver what could have been a traumatic presentation in a meaningful way. I asked questions about how the company's culture worked and wrote down their values, plucking out quirky words and language that the actors could use to deliver the brief. I then employed a television writer to script the actors carefully, involving the client throughout the scriptwriting process. The client even acted a part, which involved gently laughing at herself, which empowered the audience to reflect on their own working style and culture. The event ran like a dream, the client was happy, the staff were motivated and informed, educated and entertained. This project was successful because of excellent writing, which in turn relied on the way it correctly addressed the brief.

Brainstorming the ideas
When helping a client to prepare for a speech, I hold a brainstorming session to get the creative juices flowing. I ask questions and use a white board to record the answers. I get the key messages up on the board after establishing the main objective. What do you want to say? Are you censoring anything? Is there anything you lack the courage to say? Don't write down what you think the audience wants to hear, rather focus on the message you want to communicate.

In a one-on-one session with a client, I have a simple approach to crafting a speech. It starts with a simple structure: beginning, middle and end. We often flesh out the idea together to make some sense of the key messages. Eventually a structure appears. At this stage I film the client practising speaking the words and bringing the language to life. We play the performance back and the client might say 'I don't want to say that!' or 'That sounds awful,' or 'What I'm really trying to say is this.' He starts editing and shaping the message. We then go back to filming and he delivers the words more eloquently. I encourage clients to take a copy home, after two hours of working on the language, so they can continue to listen to what they are saying and really hone the words.

Don't be afraid to involve others in your writing. This will stimulate new ideas and will result in a more creative outcome. Another person's ideas will often provoke you to think more laterally. I often brainstorm ideas on the phone with friends all over the world (and my phone bill shows it!). I'm always interviewing people to stretch my imagination and see if I'm on the right track. Remember the brainstorming rule: there is no right or wrong answer; anything goes.

Mind mapping

Mind mapping is a note-taking method developed by Tony Buzan, author of *The Mind Map Book*. It involves drawing pictures using colour and symbols instead of taking linear notes. Start with the central topic, and draw related ideas branching out in all directions.

I often encourage clients to use this technique, particularly when they're struggling to write their material. It enables the brain to free up so you don't have to worry about the structure of what you're trying to say. It's a useful tool to get the words out and to clarify the ideas you're trying to develop.

Write from within

I recall working with a chairman on his presentation skills; in the past his speeches had been written for him, but I felt he needed to write them himself to build his confidence. We made a start and out of a conversation grew his introduction. I often encourage my clients to write their own beginnings. Don't wait for someone else to do it. You know deep down inside what you want to say.

A good writer can play with language to make words sound more powerful but the message, the ideas, and the stories still have to come from within you.

Keep your audience in mind

I always feel honoured to have an audience listen to me. Never take it for granted. I remember one of my clients saying, 'How on earth can I get passionate about writing about tax and all this dry material?' My answer was, 'Get excited about tax. How can you expect your audience to get motivated if you're not enthusiastic?'

If you're not motivated about your subject, ask yourself why. Are you the right person to deliver the speech? Do you still want to be in this job? Challenge yourself. Confidence comes from knowing and understanding your audience's needs and your subject matter.

I recall one client, a Chief Financial Officer, saying, 'The audience will be bored. They've heard it all before.' Of course they will be if you write with this thought in mind! If you make an effort to write and present the content differently and more creatively then you'll be rewarded with a motivated and responsive audience.

Keep learning

We can always learn about expressing our ideas in a more

eloquent way. One way I improved my writing was to listen carefully to the way people speak. If there's a word I don't know, I look it up in the dictionary later. Reading books has pushed my creative boundaries when writing. Stimulate your brain with other people's ideas to trigger off your thoughts.

Learn from your peers. When I attend a business lunch, I sit and really concentrate on how people are shaping their speech, or constructing their sentences. This practice helps me to understand what makes an articulate speaker.

Tell stories in your writing

> Powerful communicators use stories to captivate and maintain our attention. A well-told story has us feeling we are right there: seeing, hearing, feeling, smelling and tasting the experience. Add to that a sense of unfolding drama and we are hooked as we listen intently to find out what happens next.
>
> The part of the brain responsible for emotion also plays a central role in memory. This is why well-told stories help us to pay attention, understand, and remember information and ideas.
>
> *Peter Milligan, Executive Coach and CEO*
> *of New Generation Leaders*

The best way I know of connecting with your audience is to share your stories. Illustrate your ideas with anecdotes. Stories help the listeners to use their imaginations. When one of my favourite clients, with whom I coached for more than six months, Richard Biec was talking about his Polish ancestry in a speech, he told the following story about his parents. It's so much more powerful than simply saying, 'My parents come from Poland,' and I can still clearly remember his presentation.

'During World War II, many Polish girls were taken away to Germany to serve in munitions factories. My mother, Czesia, was 15 and had received word that the Germans were close at hand. She attempted to hide in a wardrobe. She was shaking noticeably as Nazi soldiers barged into the home and dragged her from the closet. All she can remember was the sight of shining army boots and machine guns before being taken to the munitions factory in Deutschland. There wasn't time to say goodbye.

'Around the same time my father, Jan, enlisted with the Polish army in order to provide some resistance against the German invasion. He was eventually captured by German troops and taken to a German POW camp. That was the end of action for him.

'Czesia and Jan met in 1945 and were married soon after. They became part of a large contingent of Polish immigrants to be shipped to Australia, and had to settle for any type of work they could find. We all received the best schooling because that was always important to them. They have both visited Poland once or twice since the war. When Czesia went back there the first time in 1978 she was reunited with her mother, who she hadn't seen since she was 15. It was a tearful reunion. Jan (80) and Czesia (75) are still married today.'

We remember stories because they are visual and stimulate our imagination. You don't have to tell a story to illustrate every point you make. But always use real examples to bring life to your content. Real stories give you credibility.

Personal stories create a communion with your audience. Tony Blair's 1998 history-making speech as the first British Prime Minister to address the Irish Parliament was a lesson in artfully using personal stories. He recalled his own Irish roots as he declared an end to more than 800 years of enmity between England and Ireland.

'I feel profoundly both the history in this event, and I feel profoundly the enormity of the honour that you are bestowing upon me. From the bottom of my heart, go raibh mile maith agaibh.

'Ireland, as you may know, is in my blood. My mother was born in the flat above her grandmother's hardware shop on the main street of Ballyshannon in Donegal. She lived there as a child, started school there and only moved when her father died; her mother remarried and they crossed the water to Glasgow.

'We spent virtually every childhood summer holiday up to when the troubles really took hold in Ireland, usually at Rossnowlagh, the Sands House Hotel, I think it was. And we would travel in the beautiful countryside of Donegal. It was there in the seas off the Irish coast that I learned to swim, there that my father took me to my first pub, a remote little house in the country, for a Guinness, a taste I've never forgotten and which it is always a pleasure to repeat.'

Concrete evidence or stories are an excellent vehicle to help you avoid sounding cliché when delivering speeches about your company to clients. Everyone wants to communicate how their business has integrity and honesty. But because nowadays everyone is using those buzz words, you risk sounding hackneyed and hollow. To avoid the cliché, I suggest showing your audience why and how the company has integrity. Give examples of how this plays out in the everyday running of the business. Paint the picture of what honesty and integrity looks like.

To help you focus on what the mission of your company is write a memo to yourself about the heart and soul of the operation. Give examples of how the mission is being manifested. If you are clear on this, your colleagues and employees will be clear and the impact on your audience will be more powerful.

Keep it simple
Don't forget the power of simple language. Keith Johnston, founder of Theatresports, tells actors to avoid trying to be clever. When you're clever, you often fail. My Theatresports training taught me not to be afraid of running short of words, or being unable to find the right word. There are a million ways of saying the same thing, and reaching for that elusive 'right' word only interrupts the thinking process.

Research
We research most things in life: our children's schools, which doctors to go to, where to go on holiday. We constantly gather information about many different subjects without even being aware of it. We need to do the same before we begin to write.

If you lack knowledge for your speech or presentation, read books, use the internet and find appropriate articles. Ask friends to provide you with material, or to suggest other people you could talk to; you'll be amazed at what or who they know. Email your work colleagues and ask them if they can provide material or point you in the right direction. Interview everyone in sight – what starts as a casual conversation may unearth some brilliant material that can be included in your presentation. Books, newspapers, magazines, interviews, television, the internet – make the most of as many resources as you can. Reading stretches the mind and helps you to get excited about your preparation. Always have a DVD handy to record a documentary and, if appropriate, make notes while watching the news or viewing an educational programme. Never go anywhere without notepaper and pen; you never know when the perfect opportunity will arise to research your upcoming speech.

Theodore Roosevelt carried a small library with him on his speech-making tours. Apparently he read a book every two days. I use reading as an inspiration for new ideas, and often carry a book in my bag for spare moments, especially when travelling on planes.

I did months of research before I started to work on this book. I read widely and made notes about how each theory related to my own experience. I started to formulate in my own mind what approach I wanted to take. I spoke to past and present clients about the kind of book they would buy and bother to read. Some of the answers set me off in a new direction. I interviewed many friends about their fears and concerns regarding speaking at meetings, interviews, standing up in public and giving a presentation. But they also shared their reading habits. They wanted a book that was simple to follow, with practical tips that could be applied in their lives. I spent a number of hours with the publisher, brainstorming content. It was simple but effective research.

Don't get bogged down in research or over-analysing your material. Think about what you already know about the subject and get the words down so you can expand on them later or get an editor to help. Value your thoughts and opinions and don't be manipulated by others or be afraid to speak your mind.

Structure holds it together

Ask yourself two questions:

1. What is your purpose? Do you want to inform, educate, inspire, entertain, persuade or make people laugh? Ask yourself: what am I creating here? What am I doing?
2. What is your message?

If you are clear and 'on message', then you will automatically choose clear, simple and concise communication. There will be no confusion in the mind of the listener, because there is no confusion in your mind.

Arrange your collected notes in some order. Start to organize your ideas. Consider your objective and what you want to say. Before I started writing this book I spent a number of days contemplating the order and content. Scribbling notes, collating articles I had written over the years, then eventually putting the chapter headings into some order. A speech also requires structure to hold the audience's attention. The audience needs to understand where the speech is going – if it jumps all over the place their attention will waver.

Remember the writing basics

These are some of the basics we were taught in school, but which often get lost in business writing:

- Think structure and write with logical order.
- Always check spelling, grammar and punctuation.
- Write with your target audience in mind. Who is your audience?
- Your writing must be clear and easy to read.
- Use relevant anecdotes and metaphors.
- Use active verbs.
- Use descriptive words.
- Develop your own writing style.
- Make sure your audience remembers you. Finish with a bang.

Of course, there are pitfalls to avoid when writing your speech. These include:

- being negative
- rude jokes and sexist or racist remarks
- being arrogant and putting an audience down
- apologies, such as 'I am sorry, I am so unprepared . . .'
- being cold and distant
- revealing too much at the beginning
- appearing disorganized and confused
- being boring and monotonous
- nervous gestures
- lecturing

Magical beginnings

Former British Prime Minister Tony Blair is undoubtedly one of our generation's most accomplished political orators. When Blair stepped up to the podium to deliver his final address to the Labour Party Conference in September 2006, he knew the whole country would be watching, possibly even the world. His political enemies were poised to tear apart his every word and accuse him of insincere spin. Against that backdrop, how did he begin?

'I'd like to start by saying something very simple. Thank you.'

Sheer magic. Blair chose everyday, ordinary language. He used plain, direct and simple words that weren't what we were expecting on such a monumental occasion. Rather than big, cleverly crafted words he delivered small, sincere words. And it worked.

An introduction must capture the listener's attention, and prepare their minds for what will follow, without revealing too much.
Rudolph Flesch

Have you often stared at an empty page or screen, trying to figure out how you will creatively open your speech with impact? Your responsibility is to be interesting and to engage your audience right from the start. Give your audience a reason for listening and being in the room. Make them hungry, make them excited, and arouse their curiosity. I always say to clients that it's essential to know how to begin and close your speech. Get this right before anything else and then you are on the way.

An audience decides if they like you within ten seconds. We need to put effort, time and commitment into the first few sentences. If you lose your audience at the beginning you have lost them for the entire presentation.

I often use questions, challenge the audience, and am inter-active by using an energizing exercise – one idea is to get them to stand up and move to a stranger and tell them about the highlights of their week. Use a prop to create laughter or a catchy, controversial phrase to shock, motivate or entertain.

Statistics are powerful; they have weight and substance, and, appropriately used, they can surprise the audience. Ask yourself what you can do with language to wake your audience up and grab them right from the start. Brainstorm and experiment with words. It's advisable to give yourself a reality check by rehearsing the intro in front of friends and peers – just in case.

When you are writing any speech or presentation, there's no rule that says you have to start at the beginning. If you're getting bogged down, leave the beginning until later. Write the bulk of your speech and finish with the introduction and the ending. You'll find that the beginning will practically write itself. Try it!

The first moment
There is no right way to open a speech or presentation, but it's important that the opening has impact.

The philosophy of a punchy and succinct opening applies to all public forms of communication. If you are sending a memo to staff via email you want to capture your team in the first sentence so they read on. We do not pay enough attention to the first magical moments when we write or when we speak. Many moving songs are successful because their opening lines are written from the heart and therefore we respond more. When people give an impromptu speech their beginnings are often more creative and spontaneous because emotion and feeling are involved and there is no time to worry about getting it wrong. The more impromptu speeches you give, the more practised you will become at giving a dynamic start.

Have a powerful opening planned and ready. I advise giving your listeners an outline of what they are about to hear, indicating the points you will be making during the speech.

A friend sitting in on a sales lecture related this story to me. She listened to a motivational speaker talking to an audience who were mostly in the real-estate industry. His opening apparently had them sitting on the edge of their seats. He started with the memorable line: 'Ladies and Gentlemen, there's no motivation like the winds of disaster blowing up your arse . . . houses are not selling and you are broke.' The shock tactics in this approach worked for this audience. You don't have to be cheap or lower your standards but if you know your audience well you can get away with something like this. It could be seen as crude but in the context it was perfect.

A few years ago I saw a production of Eve Ensler's play, *The Vagina Monologues*. The beginning was startling: the three actors sat on chairs staring at us in the dark. After about three minutes, one of the three said, 'You should be worried.'

This opening was different. It was confronting for the audience and it certainly had our attention.

Keep your message simple and try and identify a key idea that people will respond to. I wrote many speeches to welcome an audience when I worked in the performing arts. I recall writing a speech in the eighties when everything to do with that industry revolved around not having enough money, going without and suffering for our art. I thought about what I really wanted to say in that speech. And all I really wanted to say was that I was grateful for what we did have in the performing arts and I wanted to focus on this for once. I strung together a few succinct words around this theme, going deep inside and connecting with what really mattered to me. The speech began: 'We focus on what is missing in the arts, not on abundance.' It was a message the audience was not expecting and one they responded warmly to.

Tips for creative openings
- Share a relevant story.
- Use a powerful analogy or metaphor.
- Ask the audience a question.
- Get them laughing (but no offensive humour).
- Get your audience to interact with each other.
- Use a quote that can be easily remembered.
- Refer to current issues from the media that day. What's hot?
- Dare to be outrageous or controversial.
- Use music. Sing if you have a good voice.

What's in it for me?
At almost every public-speaking course you attend you'll hear the expression WIIFM: what's in it for me? Roger McGill, who taught presentation skills for a global organization, first told me this expression, which I have often used in my

teaching. A memorable beginning should address this question. There has got to be a reason for your audience to listen to you. Make the speech relevant to them. Why are they there and what do they need to receive?

The following list sets out one approach you might like to use when opening a speech.

- Tell the audience what you are going to talk about. 'I am here to tell you how to become an engaging public speaker.'
- Ask a question. This is a good technique to wake people up at the beginning. 'How many of you have rushed to the bathroom before giving a speech and thrown up?'
- Humanize your speech by telling them a story. 'My client Susy, a confident manager, vomited in the gutter an hour before her presentation.'
- Stun them with hard-hitting facts and statistics. 'One million people per year visit a therapist because of their phobia about speaking in public.'
- Make them laugh. 'My friend thought she was going to have to give mouth to mouth to a man who fainted before giving a speech at a conference she was organizing.'

Memorize your opening words
Trust your memory and try not to read the beginning of your speech. The audience will doubt your credibility if you read from the word go. We are often most nervous at the start of a speech, so it is vital to learn your introduction well and to thoroughly rehearse the beginning. Avoid rote learning; you need to understand the meaning behind the words as well. If you learn a speech off by heart with no room for deviation, and then you forget the words, you may panic and have no idea where you're up to.

A good idea is to have cue cards with bullet points as

security in case your memory fails, but after thorough rehearsal you'll rarely need to use them. You'll feel safe at the start of your speech if your beginning is well rehearsed. Sometimes during a coaching session I will just focus on the start to build my client's confidence.

Of course, it's a little difficult to memorize the opening of an impromptu speech. If asked to make a speech without prior warning, I sometimes scribble on an envelope from my handbag and end up glancing at the paper before I speak, but try to memorize the bullet points. The piece of paper is often my security blanket, and having it there usually means I don't need it.

When I was working for New Zealand prime minister, Helen Clark, I would often escort her to events where she was speaking. I never saw her read an opening from notes. Her words flowed from the heart, and it enabled her audience to trust in the message she was delivering.

The A list
When crafting the beginning of your speech, refer to the A list below to ensure a fantastic opening.

- **Awareness of the audience** – know what their expectations are and pay attention to their needs
- **Authority of subject** – you are the expert in your field, with a particular knowledge. Be confident that the audience is looking forward to hearing what you have to say
- **Appropriate** – is the language appropriate at the start?
- **Attitude** – inspire the participants with your positive manner
- **Authentic** – be genuine and trustworthy
- **Attraction** – the audience is looking for reasons to like you and your message

- **Anecdotes** – storytelling can be an effective way to engage the audience at the beginning of your speech
- **Awaken** – don't be afraid to draw attention to yourself by shaking up your audience
- **Aura** – the impression you create at the beginning will be remembered throughout the speech

Impact now, not later!

Advertising is similar to public speaking in that you are asking the audience to believe in your message. David Ogilvy, the advertising guru, says, 'If you screw up the introduction, the client wastes 80 per cent of their money.' Which current television commercial can you best remember? How does it begin? Why is it memorable? Think of your speech as a television commercial when you are writing and performing it. Commercials inevitably have an impact in a shorter duration because they have been well structured and well written.

Opening meetings

Many of my clients ask me how to start a meeting with meaning and gusto. One of the complaints I have from senior managers is that they feel they aren't listened to in meetings. The first question I ask is 'How do you start the meeting, how do you open it?' I sometimes spend two hours on the first five minutes of their delivery. If your intention is to entertain your staff, then take a risk and do something that is entertaining. If your purpose is to deliver bad news in an empowering way then you need to set the scene accordingly. Ask yourself this question every time: 'What response do I want in the first 30 seconds?' Think back to all the meetings you have attended – who made the most impact and why?

Passion wins every time. No matter what your message, deliver it with energy and commitment. Your body language and voice will need to be in tune with your words. If they are not, your audience will simply find something more exciting to think about while you're talking.

Endings – finishing with a bang

Let's go back to Tony Blair's address to the Labour Party Conference in 2006 to illustrate how to create an effective ending and to remind you of how important they are.

At the end of his speech, in which he was effectively taking his final bow to the party, Blair went out with this:

'Politics is not a chore. It's the great adventure of progress. I don't want to be the Labour leader who won three successive elections. I want to be the first Labour leader who won three successive elections.

'So: it's up to you. You take my advice. You don't take it. Your choice. Whatever you do, I'm always with you. Head and heart. You've given me all I have ever achieved, and all that we've achieved, together, for the country.

'Next year I won't be making this speech. But in the years to come, wherever I am, whatever I do, I'm with you. Wishing you well. Wanting you to win. You're the future now. Make the most of it.'

Short, sharp and succinct sentences are biting. It's important the audience remembers you and your key message. The last sentence can be the most striking of the entire speech. How do you want to be remembered? The ending is the opportunity to reinforce your key points. Take as much care with the end of your speech as with the beginning.

As with the beginning, learn the ending off by heart and sound like you mean every word. You have an opportunity to add value to people's lives. Don't waste that moment. Be memorable. Be sincere and be yourself. Be passionate and lively. Go out on a high.

Learn from others. Make notes of powerful endings when you listen to other speakers, like Tony Blair. Write them down so you remember them. They will inspire you to write your own with more confidence.

I sometimes tell a story at the end so the audience can remember the key messages of the presentation. Finishing with a famous quote or an excerpt from a book that is relevant to the key message can also be very powerful.

Always give your audience something to think about. Leave people feeling pleased they invested the time to listen to your presentation.

Common mistakes with endings

So you've written a great ending; a punchy final line, a great story or quote. Be aware that your delivery is also important. The following unconscious verbal and nonverbal messages can easily sabotage your grand finale.

- Negative statements. Your audience wants to feel as if the time they spent listening to you has been worth it. Finishing on a down note will lower your audience's spirits.
- Excuses. Don't apologize for what you think are the weaknesses of your speech. Saying 'I'm sorry I haven't covered everything you need to know,' only alerts your audience to something they may not have even noticed. Preparing properly for your speech should mean you don't have anything to apologize for anyway.
- Saying 'I have nothing more to say.' This is a redundant statement. If it's the end of the speech, it's obvious that's all you have to say.
- Promising a question time at the end and then running over time so it doesn't happen. If your audience has been saving up questions to ask at the end of your speech, they

will feel annoyed if they don't have the opportunity to do so.

- Avoid speeding up your pace because you are running out of time. This just means people won't be able to understand you. Thorough rehearsal will mean you know how long your speech will take and whether it fits into the allocated time.
- Dropping your energy with your voice. Stay enthusiastic and positive right till the end.
- Frowning and walking away, looking as if it's been a chore and it's a relief to finish. This behaviour will tell the audience how you expect them to react. Finish with a sunny smile and confident stance, and you help the audience to think they've just heard a great speech.

Expert help

If you are qualified to speak, then sit down and begin to write. But if you are struggling, consider paying a writer to help you to kick-start the process. I paid a high-profile comedy writer to write a speech for me once. It was an investment well made, as I was able to focus on the performance and rehearsal. We worked together on the process. I did the research, gave her my ideas and she shaped the message using her particular style of writing. The objective of the speech was to entertain the audience – and in that area I bowed to her talent.

Involving an expert can also help if you're procrastinating about getting pen to paper. It can also remove a great deal of stress. Some of my clients arrive for rehearsals without having written their speech, feeling guilty and apologetic, and the best way for them to proceed is often to pay a writer to craft the speech so they can focus on its delivery.

Of course, you may not need to pay for help; look around at the people in your own life. Capable writers surround you, in your own family, your workplace and your network of friends. Try ideas out on them and ask for feedback.

However, don't feel you need to turn to an expert every time you have to write a speech. If you know your subject well, back yourself to be able to craft it into a fantastic presentation. When you're confident about the material, you'll find the right words to say because of your excellent knowledge of the subject.

Delivering other people's material

Delivering a speech with passion is easier when you have a burning message to get across. Of course, we're sometimes asked to deliver somebody else's words. It might be that we have to fill in for another presenter, using her material, or we might be pressed for time and have to rely on a scriptwriter to prepare the speech. In this instance, your role is more like that of an actor, and your goal is to work with the playwright's text yet make it your own. You still need to make sense of the words, in order to be believable for the audience. Regard it as a challenge to use someone else's words and make it work for you. If you don't, the audience won't believe you. If you are delivering material prepared by others, it's crucial to become so familiar with it that it seems as if you'd written it yourself.

Remember that words don't necessarily have power unless they are delivered effectively. It comes back to understanding the meaning behind the words. I encourage my clients to improvise around somebody else's script or to make it their own by using personal anecdotes.

For many years I trained Lotto presenters, and I loved every moment of working with these vibrant people. I treasured this job because I was able to see the progress when the director gave the presenters an opportunity to be more involved with the material. We would workshop the Lotto draw, moving away from the script so they had to be more spontaneous. I noticed how the presenters started to free up and become more skilled at impromptu speaking. I utilized Theatresports techniques to get the presenters to improvise around the script. It requires a great deal of trust to move away from scripted words on nationwide television and yet still deliver on time when you only have a few minutes on air every Saturday night. I continue to watch the draw when I am home and still feel part of the process. Since that training project I have so much respect for any entertainer who has to keep the pace up and pay such respect to the material. They are reading material written by someone else but sound as if they created the words themselves.

TIPS ON WRITING YOUR SPEECH

Who are your audience? Why are they here? What do they want and need to know? What are their expectations? Write with your target audience in mind.

Establish your purpose. What do you want to achieve with the speech?

Have a central theme and a destination. Where do you intend to take your listeners?

Do you want to inform, persuade, entertain or a combination of all three?

Weave the last paragraph around the central message of your speech.

Think of your presentation as a conversation or a talk, not a formal speech.

Write or type your focus sentence at the top of the page, then write your title in the middle of the page and list ideas around it.

Write with images or pictures in mind. Talk in pictures.

Avoid technical jargon. A 12-year-old should be able to understand your speech.

Excite and stimulate your audience's imagination to gain their attention. What will turn them on? Share your thoughts with the audience.

7

YOUR AUDIENCE

Don't forget that your audience has rights too. They have the right to hear you clearly, see you, be moved to tears or laughter or anger by what you say, be inspired and ultimately to boo you, if they wish.
Witi Ihimaera, author

The dictionary defines 'audience' as a 'group of listeners or spectators, especially in theatre or reached by radio'. This definition can be extended: an audience includes everyone from the people in the doctor's waiting room looking at you when your mobile phone rings to dinner guests at a party. Audiences can range from one person to vast numbers of people. We have an audience in our homes, our relationships and in our work environment, as well as in structured speaking engagements. At this very moment you are my audience, listening to me speaking to you through this book.

The golden rule of managing your audience is that people will respond positively if you are authentic in your interaction with them. Your job is to make your audience comfortable and at ease so they will listen to every word you say. You must be concerned with how they are feeling.

You will inspire others if you feel inspired by what you are about to say. Imagining being on the receiving end of your speech will help you to give it your all.

Making a connection

Public speaking has changed my life and it brings me so much pleasure when I touch strangers' lives in a short time with a positive message. Ask yourself every time you present, why am I doing this? Find a reason other than financial reward. You have to speak from the heart in order to connect with your audience.

Speakers need to connect with their audiences in the first thirty seconds. The start of your speech needs to grab the audience's attention. Creating a response and building a relationship relies on you making some sort of connection, so you can then begin to communicate effectively. It's the most wonderful feeling to finish a speech and think, 'Wow, the audience and I were really in sync.' I leave on a high when this happens as the adrenaline kicks in, knowing the speech was a success because the audience was with me all the way.

> There is a difference between impressing an audience, and connecting with an audience. But once you have the connection, you can take them where you want to go.
> *Les Brown, quoted in* Secrets of Superstar Speakers

In order to perform successfully and get the message across, we need to respect and accept our audience, no matter who they are. Failing to connect with your audience can have embarrassing consequences for a speaker – I've seen people fall asleep when a speaker lacks energy or pizzazz. While we can't always control the audience's responses, we can do everything in our power to make sure people sit up and listen. As author Brian Tracy so aptly says, 'You get them to like you by showing them that it is an honour to be with them.'

I learnt some valuable lessons about the importance of the audience when I worked in the theatre. Each person coming to see the show needed to get their money's worth, or word of mouth would ensure the production didn't run for long. We owed it to the audience to get it right. They were coming night after night to watch and listen, learn, feel, be moved to tears or laughter and see their lives up there on a stage. They were paying our salaries, keeping the theatre open and the cultural arts alive. We were always grateful to our audiences for supporting our productions, and performed even if there were only a few people in the theatre. I have a newspaper clipping in a scrapbook reporting an audience of three people in a community hall in a small rural town – the show had to go on. I was very embarrassed when the media chose that moment to turn up, but we gave it our best anyway.

> To act without an audience is the same as singing in a room without any resonance . . . To act before a full and responsive audience is like singing in a hall with excellent acoustics.
> *Constantin Stanislavski*

I've worked with people who have confessed that they hate their audience and then wonder why there is no rapport. If you feel this miserable toward your listeners, I suggest you refuse the engagement. It's simply not fair to ask an audience to listen to a presenter who doesn't want to be there – if you don't care, then why should your audience? If you look at a speaking engagement as another boring or tiresome task then the result will be just that.

Encore! Encore!

When the audience wants to hear more from you, it's like nothing else on earth. I have stood up with others and cheered and stamped my feet wanting more when a speaker or singer has been brilliant. When you next give a speech think back to all these events where you've wanted to hear more, and try to analyse why these performers held your attention.

Get the audience involved

Christian Godefroy and Stephanie Barrat, in their book *Confident Public Speaking*, say the audience's ability to retain information differs depending on how the information is presented to them.

According to their research, audiences will retain the following percentage of material from the following presentation methods:

10 per cent from reading
20 per cent from listening
30 per cent from looking
50 per cent from listening and looking
80 per cent from active participation

My clients are often afraid of introducing audience participation into their speech because it involves risk, experimentation and getting involved with the people they are speaking to. It also makes some speakers feel very vulnerable.

The best way to get your audience to respond is first to gain their trust.

How to gain an audience's trust

For an audience to trust you, you must firstly trust in what you are saying and have confidence in yourself. An audience will never respond if you project a lack of confidence in yourself. Superstar speakers like Bill Clinton are in demand because they have an inner confidence when they speak.

My job is to step into the room and capture every soul.
Tony Robbins, quoted in Secrets of Superstar Speakers

Learning to trust an audience simply takes time and practice. Interact with your audience. They are not separate; they are a part of your communication, your speech or your business presentation. It has to be a two-way conversation even if you are the only one speaking. Interact with them so they are fully engaged. Communication is like a dance. It must involve movement; back and forth, a flow of energy and dialogue.

Here are some different ways to interact with an audience:

- Physically. If you are speaking to a small group, greet them individually with a warm handshake and a personal smile. If you're speaking to a larger group, greet at least a few of the audience before the presentation. This will put you at ease and generate a comfortable atmosphere.
- Verbally. When addressing the group, speak as though you're talking to a group of friends, not strangers.
- Mentally. Know in your heart that this audience wants you to succeed. They never want you to fail.
- Using content. Understand why the audience has come to hear you, and make sure the content of your speech reflects this.

- Using participation. Ask questions of your audience and get them involved at the end of your speech or during it.

What does your audience need and expect from you?
There are eight qualities that matter to me when addressing an audience:

A   Attitude
U   Unity
D   Direction
I   Involvement
E   Empathy
N   Nurturing
C   Credibility
E   Enthusiasm

Attitude
A positive attitude is the most important quality any communicator can possess. Your audience will be more attentive and energetic, and will respect you for your great outlook on life. If you're angry or upset, don't speak to an audience – the response will be negative, as your body language will ultimately give you away.

My personality is 90 per cent attitude.
Elwood N Chapman, Your Attitude is Showing

Speakers who have charisma are always positive. You can learn to have a more positive attitude in life.

Tips
- Smile and you will start to feel more positive.
- Practise communicating with a positive attitude whenever possible and you will experience remarkable results.
- Remove all negative chatter and thoughts from your mind when you speak. Every time you start to blame or put yourself down, stop – think – pause and replace it with a positive thought.
- Read and study books that explain different styles of behaviour so you can understand your moods and change habits or ask for honest feedback. How do people perceive you?

Unity

Your job is to bring your audience together so you can establish two-way communication. It's about making people feel part of a group. We need to understand why people are listening to us. What do you do in your family when you want to bring people together? You sit them down, make them feel comfortable and communicate in a caring way. What do you do in your team at work? You gather everyone around or call a meeting and empower them with a motivational message. How do you unify family and friends? You find common ground and welcome them into your home and take care of them, as you would expect to be taken care of in their homes. Our business audience is no different. Create a warm and inviting atmosphere so your audience feel as though they belong.

Tips

Ask questions and involve them. A question at the beginning is a good way to kick off. Allow questions at the end.

   Ask your audience to turn to the person sitting next to

them and discuss their point of view. You are delivering a speech but there is still room for participation, as you would expect in a business presentation. I do this often and it always works.

Plant someone in the audience to ask the first question. This gives others the confidence to ask questions as well.

Humour unifies an audience because laughter breaks down barriers. Send yourself up to make a point. You could also hire a professional actor to warm up the crowd.

Direction

You have a responsibility to take your audience on a voyage. We all want to know where we are being led in a speech. You need to direct them on a carefully mapped-out route, so they are not confused about your message. Lively communicators make the audience feel as if they matter, and that they have thought about how to communicate their message.

People always want to know there is a purpose to what they are listening to. It is a simple route: the audience needs a beginning, middle and an end to the presentation in order to understand it. Take your audience on an enjoyable voyage; let them see colourful imagery on the way, let them use their imaginations.

Tips
- Have a beginning, middle and an end to your speech.
- Give an overview at the beginning so the audience know where you are leading them.
- Summarize your key points at the end to remind them of what they have heard.
- Dream up a unique ending that is easy for your audience to remember.

Involvement

People learn best in an experiential environment. The simplest way of involving an audience is by asking questions and getting them talking so that the communication is two-way. Try to think of activities that will enhance the messages you are communicating to your audience. I interrupt most of my speeches with an interactive exercise to make a point, and to energize the audience. Improvised drama or similar creative exercises provide some light relief and help to explain a concept.

Tips

- Ask the audience to think of a story relevant to the theme of the presentation. Tell them to turn to their neighbour and share this anecdote with them.
- Introduce an energizer, get everyone up on their feet. It must be relevant to the theme.
- Hire actors to improvise or act out a scenario.
- Invite a surprise guest, and get the audience to anticipate who is turning up.
- Place a gift on each chair that will stimulate discussion to bring home a point so people start chatting to each other before you start.
- Ask people to look under their chairs for a sticker you have put there earlier. Invite the winners up to the lectern to receive a gift that is relevant to the theme of the speech or to tell a story. At a successful film premiere, prizes were given to people standing on stars in the carpet pattern. A great idea!

Empathy

Empathy is the power of understanding and imaginatively entering into another person's feelings. This is one of the most essential tools in communication. Never put down, blame or judge your audience. The audience will feel safe and trust you if you show that you empathize with them. Share your experiences so they will be in tune with you.

We learn to be empathetic by listening and observing others. It is an empowering skill and it is especially necessary in business if you are in a senior or leadership role.

Tips

- Make sense of what you've heard, putting it into your own words to show you have understood. For example, if someone says, 'I'm burnt out', you could say, 'You must be feeling exhausted.' Be sure to speak in your own words rather than parroting what they've said. People need to know you are hearing them.
- Observe people's body language for unspoken messages about how they're feeling.
- Take time to stop and to listen to people.

Nurturing

It's the presenter's responsibility to nurture the audience, to take care of them no matter what the subject matter. I don't mean babying them – rather, fostering people as you go along. Enable them to learn. Deepak Chopra, the famous author, is a master at nurturing his audience – I remember sitting in an auditorium fascinated by his caring nature as he walked the length of the stage. The warm tone in his voice made me feel as though he was talking directly to me.

> The audience provides our spiritual acoustics, like a sounding board – returning to us living, human emotions.
> *Constantin Stanislavski*

Tips

- Nurture yourself first then attend to the audience. You are no use to anyone unless you pay attention to your own wellbeing.
- Speak with a caring tone in your voice.
- Kindness doesn't cost, so be generous with it.
- One way of showing that you care is to stay around after your speech is over to listen to people's questions and engage with them.
- Check your audience are physically comfortable – speak to the venue organizers before the event. See Chapter 13 on setting the stage for further ideas.

Credibility

Your audience needs to believe you from the moment you open your mouth. You are the expert in your field and that's why you are speaking to this audience. Without credibility your messages will have no impact. Don't be afraid to let your audience know why you are the best person to speak to them on a topic. For example, if you're speaking about sales techniques because you've been your company's top sales rep for the last year, make sure that the audience know this either through your speech or through the person who introduces you. This gives the audience a reason to trust you and your message.

Your reputation is important. Being introduced at the beginning of your presentation is vital as it establishes your credibility. The MC needs to know if there is any information you would like told to the audience before you start speaking.

Tips

- Provide the person introducing you with relevant, up-to-date material and credentials well in advance. Let him know how you'd like to be introduced.

- Don't be afraid to tell people about your skills. What is your claim to fame? How will people know if you don't tell them?
- If possible try to meet the person introducing you so she gets a sense of who you are. You can also provide her with anecdotes about you in a face-to-face meeting.

Enthusiasm

Enthusiasm is essential to wake up any audience and keep their interest. You cannot have too much passion. I ask every new client 'what are you passionate about?' This forms the basis of my approach in coaching so I can tap into what matters to them. Depriving your audience of your enthusiasm robs them of any relationship with you. Audiences will forgive you almost anything if you are wholehearted and share your inner beliefs.

Business success isn't just about getting the job done. It's about inspiring commitment and creating an achievement-based culture that turns what can be ordinary into something extra-ordinary.
Glenys Coughlan, CEO NBPR

Who are your favourite speakers? I guarantee they display eagerness and zest. Enthusiasm comes from loving what you do, so be cheerful and eager when presenting to a group.

Tips
- Practise being positive in your private life and it will spill over into your presentation and professional life.
- Look at the company you keep and surround yourself with enthusiastic people. It rubs off.

- Talk about something you are passionate about. If your material is dry, boring and dull to you then how is your audience expected to get excited about it? Tell stories that fire you up.
- Confident posture, a smile, energy and a lively voice tell your audience you are enthusiastic.

Warming up the crowd

Many years of experience working as a professional MC have taught me how important it is to read the audience carefully. It is crucial to be adaptable and flexible with a crowd. Don't be afraid of things going wrong. Two-way communication is about mutual understanding. What is your audience feeling and thinking? What is the mood or atmosphere telling you? Are they relaxed, shy, receptive, defensive, angry or cynical?

Great MCs are particularly skilled in interacting with an audience. They do this with charm, wit and humour. They are successful partly because of the amount of research they do before each assignment.

Some suggestions for warming up the crowd include:

- Bring spot prizes to give away, such as a book, voucher or movie ticket. Make it relevant to the presentation's theme.
- Competitions can be fun – ask a question and have a prize for the winner.
- Get the audience to do a Mexican wave. (Not every audience will like the sound of this so think carefully about this one!)

Heckling

Even the best presenters have to deal with hecklers at times – people who either disagree with what you're saying, or just want to disrupt the speech or show off. Don't take it personally and, above all, stay calm. The rest of the audience is usually annoyed by hecklers, and you may find that someone else in the audience asks them to be quiet on your behalf. Some of my strategies for dealing with hecklers are:

- In the first instance, try to ignore them. If it's a one-off comment that doesn't merit a response, continue with your presentation. Break eye contact with the person. If the audience can see you're not paying any attention to the heckler, neither will they.
- If the heckler is intent on attracting your attention to make his point, I don't recommend trying to heckle back. You'll just get drawn into a slanging match. Stay polite, and the audience will be on your side.
- You could try a comment such as, 'We have a lot of material to cover and I'd rather not get off track, so how about at the break we get together and talk about this then.' Hopefully, the heckler will understand this as a request to tone it down. Another approach is to acknowledge their point of view with a comment such as 'That's one way to look at it,' or 'I can see why you might think that, but consider looking at it this way.' If they really persist, ask the audience, 'Is anyone else having difficulty with this point?' If the answer is no, suggest to the heckler that you continue the conversation during the break.
- If the heckler is getting some laughs from the rest of the audience and it's not at your expense, go along with it, within reason of course. The audience might even think you planted the heckler to help liven up your presentation.
- If you're really concerned about heckling, ask the event organizers to appoint a 'bouncer' and discuss what action you'd like them to take should heckling get out of control. This is rather heavy-handed however, and does make you

look defensive – but if your subject matter is contentious, you might like to consider this approach.

- If a couple of people are talking through your presentation, ask them a question or just stop and wait for them to finish. If someone starts talking on a mobile phone, ask him politely to leave the presentation and carry on his conversation outside.

TIPS ON MANAGING YOUR AUDIENCE

Credibility is crucial – let your audience know why you've been asked to speak to them. Your MC can also do this for you.

Your audience wants you to succeed – they're on your side. What do you want to achieve with the speech?

Energize your audience. Consider an interactive activity at the beginning or part way through your speech.

Gifts and prizes can be a fun icebreaker.

Smile! Your enthusiasm will be contagious – show you're enjoying yourself and your audience will too.

Look at your audience, not the floor. Build rapport by making eye contact.

Take risks – let your audience know who you are and what you stand for. Be prepared to step outside your comfort zone.

Ask experienced trainers for help. Borrow exercises and activities that have a proven record in order to enliven your presentation.

8

WARMING UP

Until you value yourself, you won't value your time.
Until you value your time, you will not achieve anything with it.
Vijay Eswaran

Warming up helps to focus the mind and body on the task ahead.

Completing a warm-up before a presentation will ensure that you are concentrating on the right things, your vocal cords are ready for action and you are relaxed and confident about the speaking engagement. Just as you wouldn't go for a run without first warming up your muscles, public speakers don't perform without first ensuring that they are ready to give 100 per cent from the very beginning of the presentation.

On the few occasions where I haven't taken the time to warm up properly, I have been unhappy with my performance. If you're not ready to perform before starting your speech, it will take the crucial first minutes of your presentation before you really get into the swing of things, and by then, you may have lost the audience's attention.

Take a lesson from the sports stars

In my view, the haka performed by the All Blacks before a test match is the most powerful public warm-up that integrates body, voice, mind and spirit. The players get so fired up during this ritual. Former All Black Stu Wilson recalls the importance of the haka to the team's pre-match routine.

'We knew we were likely to get smashed if we didn't warm up properly. If the haka was done well, I could tell the boys were going to play well. The opposition were in trouble. The haka put them at a disadvantage – they sometimes turned their back on us because they felt challenged. The haka gave us instant recognition – it was like the opening of the performance, just like the opening line in a speech.'

There are many similarities between theatre and sports. Shelley McMeeken, former CEO of Netball New Zealand, comments, 'One of the compelling things about netball is its unpredictability. It's like unprescribed theatre such as Theatresports where the athletes [actors] are part of an unpredictable story line.' Sportspeople wouldn't dream of competing without adequate preparation; it becomes part of their routine. They know that they don't perform to the best of their ability if their minds and bodies are not ready for action.

Shelley describes her warm-up routine for press interviews. 'For us to be successful we have to win on and off the court. The players warm up before a big game and equally I warm up prior to a press conference or interview by visualizing what tactics I may have to counter. Our Silver Ferns don't go on unprepared when they represent our organization and nor should I.'

Do what works for you

Warm-ups are very personal – try different activities until you find something that clicks. Sometimes I listen to upbeat music if I am giving an early-evening speech at cocktail hour.

I have even been known to dance around the conference room with technicians and hotel staff in the room. The goal is to get the blood flowing and the brain focused on the presentation. Experiment and talk to friends about their warm-up routines.

One of the more unusual warm-up routines I've seen is that advocated by Ross Foreman, one of Australasia's most successful auctioneers. I co-facilitated a workshop with him training auctioneers to perform more effectively. Auctioneers are very aware of the need to warm up before performing because of the stress they place on their voices. The auction process is very theatrical and relies on a powerful perform-ance with a strong voice and the familiar fast rhythm. He used to ask each auctioneer to hold a chair as though it was a set of bagpipes and to walk around the room making rhythmical sounds! Taking people out of their comfort zones in a non-threatening way broke down barriers and helped to build their confidence. Ross also liked to use poetry and excerpts from plays as part of the auctioneers' warm-up programme. The participants would stand outside under the trees and practise projecting their voices. We also used improvisation and theatre-style vocal exercises.

I remember one excellent auctioneer who was named Auctioneer of the Year several years in a row in Australia. One year when he didn't win the title, he confessed that he hadn't warmed up his voice or been through his standard set of relax-ation exercises before the competition.

Routine

We prepare for most things in life. We have rituals before we go to work, go to the gym, cook a meal. Brushing our teeth in the morning is a part of preparing for the day. Stretching before exercising is another preparation.

Incorporate small exercises into your pre-presentation routine and always warm up before you speak. If you are reluctant to do this, ask yourself why. Is it because you don't know what to do or can't find a quiet room or space? Perhaps you feel stupid or believe it won't make a difference. Maybe you can't be bothered. With positive self-talk and a commitment to delivering a first-class presentation to your audience, you will find ways to deal with these doubts.

I often warm up in the venue one hour before a speech. If working with a client, I make sure I am also there to help them warm up. Find someone to support you during your warm-up exercises to make sure you do them.

Warm-ups can be a combination of any or all of the following activities: going to the gym, walking, singing, meditating, praying, using positive self-talk, practising a few yoga postures or a warm-up of your own choice before the performance. There are suggestions later in this chapter of particular exercises you might like to try, but the main thing is to find a warm-up that works for you, that you feel comfortable with, and gets you physically and mentally ready to give a great presentation.

Don't just warm up for a public speech. Even interviews and salary negotiations are performances which require you to be on your toes and focused. Make limbering up a habit; it will eventually start to become a ritual for you until you cannot imagine speaking to a group without going through your routine.

How long should I take?

Warm-ups can last from five minutes to one hour, depending on how much time you can spare or how experienced you are at speaking in public. Make an appointment with yourself to do some kind of physical and vocal practice before your next presentation, even a quick walk around the block – anything to get the blood pumping.

Ask a friend or colleague to monitor you if you are struggling to be disciplined. Set up a buddy system so you can return the favour. Motivate them and help them to remove some of the stress around their presentation.

Privacy

People often ask, 'Where can I warm up without people watching?' Find any quiet place. Most of my warm-ups are carried out in the hotel or conference centre's bathroom.

I remember being desperate to find a quiet room for a client to warm up in before an Annual General Meeting in a hotel. We discovered a few metres of space in between the kitchen and the major speaking room; the floor was on a slant so it was a challenge. I felt like we were in a tiny cupboard but it was sufficient despite the fact we later learnt that the chef could hear our humming sounds!

Some of my clients over the years have giggled their way through a warm-up routine prior to delivering a speech or presentation in a rehearsal. I remember an Australian Chief Executive looking at me with an expression of horror saying: 'There is a lot I will do for you, Maggie, but that is going too far!' I had simply been asking him to practise the horse-lips exercise, which relaxes the muscles in the face and jaw. The exercise involves blowing air through the mouth, and sounds like blowing raspberries on a baby's tummy. It is a tremendous release and more then most other facial exercises seems to make people free up and release tension in the face.

I understand that he felt a bit silly, because he was afraid of looking stupid. However, after a few months of practising this before presentations, the client saw on film that getting rid of tension from the body and relaxing the muscles in the face had drastically improved his public speaking. He now makes a warm-up a compulsory component of his public speaking routine – in private of course!

Suggestions for your warm-up routine
Breathing
We often take breathing for granted, yet the quality of our breath determines the quality of our speech.

Try to avoid shallow breathing, which occurs when you raise your shoulders but your lungs aren't given enough room to expand. Shallow breathing means we don't get enough air to finish a sentence. If you have to stop for breath in the middle of a sentence, it is likely that you're not breathing deeply enough. The goal is to speak so your sentences flow from one to the other.

On the breath are carried our words – and with it our intent – the quality of what we say.
Sallie-Ann Stones, yoga teacher

In yoga every movement is led by the breath. Many years ago I attended a two-day workshop with one of the world's top yoga teachers, Desikachar, author of the classic yoga text, *The Heart of Yoga*. He says, 'There are many interpretations of the word yoga that have been handed down over the centuries. One of these is to come together, to unite. Another meaning of the word yoga is to tie the strands of the mind together.'

I love the latter expression; knowing the meaning behind the word 'yoga' helps to understand why it can be a helpful tool in your warm-up routine.

Every time you experience stage fright, breathe deeply in and out and eventually you will relax. I practise yoga breathing most days, especially before teaching.

Sallie-Ann Stones, yoga teacher, talks about the benefits of yoga in her life: 'The practice of yoga has given me a greater understanding of my possibilities and most importantly, myself, my capabilities and my limitations. It has been a tool of growth – as my body has become stronger and more flexible and re-aligned itself from past habits, I have observed that my mental and emotional states have followed suit. As my breath has deepened, so has my thinking. As my energy has increased, so has my interest in life. As I've become more comfortable and at ease in my body it has become more natural and easy to stand up and be who I am.' Do consider attending a yoga class to improve your breathing habits.

If you have difficulty breathing, I highly recommend Dinah Bradley's book, *Hyperventilation Syndrome*, to increase your understanding of your breathing patterns. Learning to breathe correctly will enable you to release the stress in your body. I often practise these exercises when I am tired or between client sessions to get more oxygen to my brain and to feel rejuvenated.

Exercise
Stand with your feet shoulder-width apart and place the palms of your hands on your lower abdomen. Close your eyes, inhaling your breath through your nose, expanding your abdomen. Raise your arms, moving them outward and above your head. Hold for a count of five, and then exhale slowly, breathing through your nose, lowering your arms. Repeat five times.

Exercise

Start by sitting comfortably, with your spine straight and your eyes and mouth gently closed. Relax your head and shoulders; relax your face and your jaw. Become aware of the flow of your own natural breath, in and out of the nostrils, without controlling or changing it in any way, just observing it and watching. Continue this until your whole mind is full of just breathing in and breathing out.

Bring your awareness to your abdomen. Imagine you have a balloon in your belly and when you breathe in fill this balloon with air. Hold the breath there, in your belly, and feel as though you are absorbing the breath deep inside yourself. If you have a particular area of pain or discomfort, imagine you are sending the breath there. Hold it only as long as you comfortably can, then release the breath. When breathing out, also release any tensions and any physical, mental or emotional negativity.

Continue for several breaths. Simply observe your natural flow of breath – see how subtle your breath has become. Notice any changes within yourself – your physical and mental well-being.

Exercise

I recommend a book called *The Power of Speech* by Marie Stuttard, which is full of simple, practical advice. She suggests the following breathing exercise.

'Take a deep breath through the nose, then start counting aloud – one, two, three . . . Go as far as is comfortable, speaking clearly and distinctly. Don't slur your words. A woman should get to around seventeen. A man – with a larger lung capacity – should make twenty or more. This simple exercise gives you a good idea of how efficient your breathing is.'

Get moving to release tension

Tension in the body when speaking is largely the result of not doing a warm-up. It's not enough just to rely on the message and words you're delivering – your body has to look as if it believes the words coming from your mouth. Where is the tension in your body?

> The fastest way to still your mind is to move your body.
> *Gabrielle Roth, dance theatre artist*

We need to get our blood and oxygen flowing to wake up. We cannot expect our listeners to be alert if we are sluggish. Fresh air is free and energizes your body. Surrendering tension invigorates your performance. What does it really mean to let the tension go? How do you like to let go? It is different for every person. For me, dancing, running on a beach, meditating, singing and laughing are all ways that I let go.

I try to spend five minutes outside of the air-conditioned training room between clients; it makes all the difference to my energy levels. Even five minutes outside peps up your body and gives you a lift.

Any movement will help you to focus. Practise your golf swing or your tennis serve. Use exercises you enjoy; don't allow it to become a chore.

> Tension is one of the absolute enemies of acting.
> *Stella Adler*

Many of you will play sport and have your own particular warm-up. What do you do to warm up before delivering a presentation? Make up your own routine that you can easily remember and structure it accordingly. It doesn't matter if you walk, move, dance or stretch, just get into a regular habit of moving.

Exercise

Start from your head and work down to your shoulders then to your arms, chest, hips, legs and feet. Move each body part, slowly rolling and stretching. Make soft gentle fluid movements that make you feel more relaxed.

Exercise

Ben Cole, who teaches public speaking in London to film actors and directors at the National Film School, talks about what happens when we panic and stop moving easily. 'There is a ball and socket joint at the top of the spine and you can't think clearly unless you are moving it.' He suggests that ten seconds before you speak, stand in front of the audience, start to move your head slightly, looking at the audience and making eye contact. Breathe deeply, wait for the right words to come out. Don't rush into speaking before you're ready. Don't make obvious movements, but slowly and naturally ease yourself into a comfortable speaking position instead of keeping your head still.

Exercise

If you suffer back pain, try the following. Lie on your back and bring both of your knees to your chest. Gently squeeze your legs. Move slowly from side to side with no great effort. This will massage your back and will stretch your lower-back muscles.

Releasing tension in the voice and face

Chapter 4 has many suggestions for improving and maintaining your voice. Here are some exercises for warming up the face and vocal cords before your presentation.

Exercise

Gargle a glass of water while singing a scale in the back of your throat as loudly as you can.

Exercise

To release tension in the mouth, try this horse-lips exercise. Blow air out through your mouth, as if you are blowing raspberries on a baby's tummy. You might prefer to be somewhere private when you try this one! Loose relaxed lips are what we are aiming for as opposed to tight ones.

Exercise

Here's another exercise for releasing tension in your face. Let your tongue sit comfortably in your mouth, and blow some air through your lips in a repetitive motion. Now add some sound and increase the volume. Your face may tingle when you do this.

Exercise

Loosen your jaw with the following exercises. Open your mouth and move your jaw from right to left. Open your mouth wide then close. Pretend you are yawning. Repeat.

Exercise

These tongue twisters will help to sharpen your diction. Repeat each phrase five times.

   Unique New York
   Red leather yellow leather

Red lorry yellow lorry
Will you wait for William and Willy?
She sells seashells on the seashore
Around the rugged rocks the ragged rascal ran.

Exercise

To improve resonance in your voice, try humming for three minutes or until your lips tingle, remembering to breathe. Many opera singers hum before a performance. You can even hum in the car, although it's preferable to set aside time to perform all exercises closer to the time you are actually speaking.

Exercise

Sing your favourite song. You are exercising the mouth, lips, tongue, jaw and facial muscles, as well as your vocal cords. Singing also makes you feel good. No need to get hung up on staying in tune; choose a song you enjoy.

Exercise

Reading aloud is an excellent way to warm up your vocal cords. Practise reading as if your audience was across the table, across the room, then across the street.

Warming up the mind

Concentrate on staying positive before your presentation, trying to remove all negative thoughts from your mind. Let go of all judgements you have about yourself and your audience before you stand up and speak. Release any preconceived ideas about the event that's about to happen. If you resent your boss, for example, because she has insisted you make a speech when you don't want to – let go of that thought and attitude. You don't need it and it will only hinder the quality of your performance.

> It is none of my business what anyone thinks of me.
> *Anonymous*

Chapter 11 on transforming fear with self-belief has a comprehensive section on using visualization and affirmations to prepare your mind for speaking in public.

Joanna Clarke, a singer, says 'to truly warm up your voice you need to be focused and to be focused you need to have let go of any thoughts that will impair you from warming up well.'

Exercise
Try listening to a relaxation CD for a week leading up to an important speech. Take an iPod with you to the venue and select music according to your needs. Classical music calms me before a speech and stops me worrying about the outcome. If I'm tired I select something more upbeat.

Exercise
Learn about meditation and try to incorporate it into your daily routine. Yoga teacher Sallie-Ann Stones says:

'We often meditate spontaneously when we are walking, fishing, day-dreaming . . . With today's life being so fast and full, reaching the state of relaxed concentration required for meditation becomes more and more difficult. Our minds become jammed with to-do lists, worry lists, should-have, would-have, could-do lists! Trying to bring the mind under control is like trying to tame the wind. The practice of meditation gives us a simple technique with which to step over this babbling mind – to a place of quiet observation. A place to rest from our mental chatter – where we can become the observer of our own mental processes, in a place of clarity and insight.'

There are many forms of meditation techniques – pick one and practise it regularly.

A sample warm-up programme

1. Stretch your body out, by dancing or jogging to music. Try a few yoga stretches or walk around the block. Get the heart going!
2. Align your body – imagine a piece of string running through your head, down the back of the neck and down your spine. Turn your head gently to the left, back to the centre, then to the right. Repeat ten times.
3. Roll your shoulders gently forward and back, then pull your shoulders up to your ears then relax. Repeat each action ten times.
4. Control your breathing – put a hand on your stomach, breathe in deeply through your nose all the way to your hand. Keep your shoulders relaxed.
5. Relax. Breathe in through your nose then breathe out through your open mouth. Pause. Repeat, making an 'ahhh' sound on the exhalation. Pause. Be aware of releasing any tension in your body. Breathe slowly, so as not to hyperventilate, then on the next exhalations, let out an easy laugh, then a 'hmmmm' sound, then hum up and down the scale.
6. Have a gargle in the bathroom. Stand tall. Breathe easy.
7. Warm up your face. Screw your face up and vigorously chew on a piece of imaginary gum. Massage your face. Vibrate your lips like a horse, making a 'ppppprrrrr' sound. Try the following sounds:
   • ptk ptk ptk ptk
   • bdg bdg bdg bdg
   • ing ah ing ah ing ah ing ah

8. Tongue Twisters. Try some of the following:
   - Little Lillian, living by the lily pond, lets lazy lizards lie along the lily pads.
   - Zena, the zenith zebra, lives life with zestful zeal.
   - Lips tongue tip of the teeth (repeat five times).
   - Articulatory agility is a desirable ability manipulating with dexterity the tongue, the palate and the lips.
9. Close your eyes and visualize yourself giving your presentation. Visualize being introduced, walking to the podium, acknowledging the audience, enjoying delivering your speech, seeing the audience enjoying listening to it, hearing the rousing applause and walking off the stage after a successful speech.
10. Use positive self-talk and affirmations, such as 'The audience want to listen to me.'
11. Enjoy yourself.

TIPS ON WARMING UP

Set up a regular time before your speech to warm up in a quiet place.

Turn off your mobile phone.

Use music to relax and energize yourself during your warm-up routine. An iPod can be handy.

Get out of the office or the venue where you're speaking and breathe in some fresh air.

Take long deep breaths until you feel your body relaxing.

9

THE REHEARSAL

The rehearsal is the place to take risks and to find out how far you can go. You must consider it is the safest place for you to push yourself and make a fool of yourself. Practise and prepare for the rehearsal before you arrive. Don't come to the rehearsal and start doing your homework.
Michael Hurst, actor and director

A rehearsal is an opportunity to try out ideas and a time to test yourself. Bad rehearsals can be frustrating but they make you go home and work harder. I have seen actors and people in business weep during a rehearsal from sheer frustration – better it happens at the rehearsal than during your presentation. These experiences can make you try new ways and make you more determined to get it right.

Double your failure rate in a rehearsal – it is OK to make mistakes. A satisfactory rehearsal gives you a sense of confidence and makes you feel positive about your upcoming speech. When you've gone through your content enough times to know you know your stuff, you'll feel calm and prepared when it comes to the real thing.

Over the years I have heard so many clients say, 'I can't

rehearse, I'm not ready and I haven't got the time.' These are excuses! Rehearsals help you to get ready for the big event.

Avoid procrastination

Rehearse until you get it right. No cutting corners, no tricks, no winging it on the day. Never delay or cancel a rehearsal. Even the most experienced and high-profile presenters rehearse when it matters.

> Practice doesn't make perfect. Perfect practice makes perfect.
> *Vince Lombardi, quoted in* Present Yourself!

I have run through speeches at the last minute when clients have left it to the eleventh hour to write their speeches. Sometimes they haven't even had time to read the speech written for them. This last-minute call to me gives the person some support, but it can be stressful as it's not the best way to rehearse. If you're one of these people who leaves it to the last minute, bring someone in to critically assess and support you but do not have unrealistic expectations of yourself.

Don't wing it

So many people over the years have told me that they wing their speeches. If you do this, you run the risk of letting yourself down, knowing you could have done better. It's not a pleasant feeling knowing that the audience didn't get their money's worth. Your integrity will also suffer as a result. So rise to the challenge, prepare well and rehearse your speech, and whatever the outcome, you'll be able to stand tall and say, 'I did my best.'

Learn from the theatre process

My work in professional theatre taught me that the audience must come first. An audience will never know the sacrifice and time investment made in your speech, and this is how it should be. They are the focus and they deserve a fresh, powerful performance from you.

> You know the words, you know the business, you know the story, you know the moves. And you know everybody else's words and moves too. And yet you have to give the illusion that you are doing it and thinking it for the first time.
> *Peter Barkworth, author of* About Acting

Can you imagine an actor performing without a rehearsal? It just wouldn't happen.

Attitude

Bring a positive attitude to a rehearsal. Leave all negative thoughts and feelings outside the room. Even if you are practising in front of just one person you need to be in a positive frame of mind. We are more creative when we are positive and more responsive to criticism. We all too often program our brain for failure before we even start. Think positive thoughts all the way through rehearsal and you will be amazed at how confident you will feel. Worrying before or during a rehearsal will not help you to prepare for your performance. Ask any professional sports achiever about this.

If you're rehearsing with a team, be supportive and help each other to be positive. We can become overly engrossed in our own performance but we need to be aware of others in the rehearsal and consider our attitudes toward them.

Giving feedback in the rehearsal

Remember first to give a positive comment about something the person is doing well. Then you can move on to constructive criticism, giving the person the information needed to improve the speech. People can be at their most vulnerable during rehearsals, especially when a tutor or speech coach has been hired to critique them. It is not easy to be given feedback in front of others, especially by a stranger.

Be very specific with feedback and give the positives first. Many training schools suggest following the Commend, Recommend, Commend sequence. See Chapter 18 on evaluating your performance for more tips on giving constructive feedback.

How many rehearsals do I need?

The number of rehearsals you choose will depend on your expertise in public speaking, your availability and your knowledge of the material being delivered.

I urge clients to set aside at least four rehearsals for a major speech. I sometimes start thinking about my speech at least five months prior if it is a large business audience. This helps my confidence and allows me to be more creative so when I sit to write some notes I know exactly where I want to take my audience and what I want to say. One rehearsal is never sufficient.

The read-through

In the theatre actors have a read-through when they first come together, then begin acting at the second rehearsal without their script in their hands. During this second rehearsal, actors arrive knowing their lines – if they don't they find themselves in big trouble, having let down the cast and wasted the director's time. After four to five weeks, they have a dress rehearsal and a technical rehearsal.

In business I follow the same procedure with my clients and educate them to change their ways if this is not their current routine. It always pays off.

Timing

I used to be notorious for going over time in my speeches, getting the royal wave from the organizer telling me kindly to wrap it up. When you're first asked to speak at an engagement, make sure you find out how long you will be expected to speak for. I'm always amazed when people forget to ask this question – it is fundamental to the planning, writing and rehearsing process.

When rehearsing, time your speech or ask someone else to act as timekeeper. Be very disciplined; twenty minutes can feel like two hours if you haven't actually timed yourself. If your speech is longer than an hour, consider giving your audience a short break. Never go over time as it can be seen as disrespectful unless your audience is asking for more and time permits.

The organizers of the Oscars send each nominee an egg timer so they can practise their two-minute acceptance speech. Not a bad idea; it's easier then using a watch when you are practising alone.

Filming your speech

Recording your speech during a rehearsal is an excellent way to see yourself as the audience will see you. It's an opportunity to notice your hand gestures, your speech inflections and to be aware of how confident you sound. I film all rehearsals so my clients can see their progress and take away a recording of the presentation to continue working on its content. The camera doesn't lie.

Visualize your performance

Visualize the audience; see their faces and imagine yourself at the venue. Let your imagination help you in your rehearsals for major speeches or presentations. When I'm rehearsing at home, I see the venue in my mind, see the audience, and imagine their response to my speech. See Chapter 11 for more information on how to visualize your speech.

The dress rehearsal

Try to run through your final rehearsal in the venue where you'll be speaking. Can your audience see you from where they are sitting? Can they hear you? Are you projecting your voice sufficiently? Are your key messages clear? Are you running over time? Are you dressed appropriately and wearing the clothing that you'll wear on the day? Better to find out during the rehearsal that the new shoes you bought are too tight and will distract you from your delivery than on the day.

A crucial element of the dress rehearsal is to ensure that all technology is working as you expect. Don't forget to check the position where you intend to deliver your presentation or speech. Are you blocking the screen from the audience?

Another important thing to check is whether a translator or a signer for the deaf will be participating in your presentation. This could well change your performance so you must include it in your rehearsal.

I learned this lesson in early 2006 when I was asked to speak at an event for a visiting Chinese government delegation. I hadn't thought to ask if there would be a translator, or indeed whether the visitors had a good understanding of English. I froze when I realized that I would be working with a translator, who would repeat in Mandarin my every sentence. I knew this would completely alter my presentation.

Luckily I managed to rescue the situation by improvising

and abandoning my notes, as well as adopting a larger than usual dose of wit, theatrics and humour. But let this be a lesson to all of us to inform ourselves fully so we can rehearse properly right from the start.

Business pitches

A large part of my current work involves helping to prepare teams of people for successful business pitches. The biggest problem I face with business-pitch rehearsals is when one person hasn't come prepared for the rehearsal. Everyone needs to come to the rehearsal having done their homework even if their speech is only for two minutes.

The general rules of rehearsal already discussed also apply to business pitches. Run through your material so you are fully prepared at home or somewhere quiet. It is the time invested in rehearsing that will make that final performance credible.

You'll be more likely to win the business account if you and your team have a practice run. Work out exactly where you will all be sitting or standing. Choreograph handovers between presenters, practise every move so it comes together smoothly.

Winning a training tender for a global organization in the early nineties was a turning point in my career. When I got the opportunity to pitch for this business, I decided to give it my all. I spent months rehearsing in front of friends who work in business and who are public-speaking coaches in their careers. I practised until I was satisfied. The investment in time was enormous but paid off as I won the contract and it led to future business opportunities.

What happens when we don't rehearse business pitches?

Cues are missed, lines are fluffed, documents are not ready to satisfaction, the team is disconnected and mistakes are made with technology when we don't rehearse. We must not waste an audience's time even if that audience is made up of only three people. The client always makes an assumption that your content will be appropriate for their business but the way you present as a team is what sometimes ultimately determines the outcome.

> Stamina, balls and confidence. You've got to just keep going.
> *Whoopi Goldberg, performer*

Over the years I have seen teams lose an opportunity to bring in a million-dollar job for their companies simply because of not rehearsing well in advance.

Who is your rehearsal director?

Every business rehearsal needs a director to pull the pitch together and get results. The rehearsal director is the person who gets the ball rolling, cues people in, assigns tasks and notices when things aren't running as they should. Someone needs to set an appropriate mood in the rehearsal. This is the job of the director. Rehearsing five top business executives pitching for a 100 million pound business deal remains a highlight of my work in the UK.

This engineering company in 2007 had been working for months on their pitch. The content was well-researched and ready, the PowerPoint presentation of a decent standard and the corporate DVD one of the best I've seen.

But a consultant hired by the company to win the pitch, Will Wesson, sensed failure without some radical overhauling of the style and manner in which the pitch was to be delivered.

I was called in at the eleventh hour.

They were talented men who knew their business well but, as a group, their performance was unconvincing.

I got straight to work. They went straight into rehearsal.

We rehearsed individually and in a group over a five-day period. We filmed every rehearsal to look for strengths, weaknesses and signs of improvement. We did a run-through before the board of the company and the CEO to get their critical feedback. We even talked about the kind of suits and colours of shirts, ties and shoes that each man would wear so as to finesse the look of their presentation.

The Managing Director Mike remembers the five days like this:

'A few of the team were way outside of their "comfort zone" but, as the preparation and rehearsals progressed, they became comfortable, assured and even began to look forward to the event.

'Warm up exercises were an experience to behold – five grown men blowing raspberries at each other, chanting rhymes and doing breathing exercises. If only our wives could have seen us – they wouldn't have believed it!

'It all added to a tremendous sense of having a shared goal, working as a team and being prepared for a "business critical" presentation.'

The pitch seemed to go really well but I had to wait three months to hear if they had won the lucrative deal.

My mobile phone was the bearer of good news. A text from Mike read: 'We did it!'

One of the men, Raj, also gave me some feedback on the difference structured rehearsing made.

'I remember how Maggie would always manage to focus on the positives in an individual's ability to present, but also firmly advise of the specific areas of improvement required.

'We arranged to meet individually with Maggie before the team would engage collectively again.

'My next session was a one to one where I was taught posture, the importance of body language and the need for my oration to be toned down in order to gain maximum impact.

'The one to one was a practical and pragmatic learning point for me. I remembered the key tips and wanted to impress.

'In the next session, the team was filmed. If anyone has come across this video nasty, then I would be happy to provide recompense for its safe and timeous destruction.

'In all seriousness, by the end of the session, I was making a conscious effort to tone down my voice, but impress upon my tone when wanting to make some key points and trying hard to stay still and use my hands as positive language.'

TIPS ON RUNNING A GREAT REHEARSAL

Make a time. Where, when, who and how often? I often phone my client and say 'let's begin'. It just takes some motivation and structure to get you started.

Be prepared before you arrive for your rehearsal. Know what it is you want to say. Run through your speech or presentation before you turn up to rehearse.

Concentrate and focus throughout the rehearsal and put other commitments out of your mind. Turn off your mobile phone.

Be in control of the technology. Who is responsible for it and do they know what to do? Practise with the technology long before the rehearsal otherwise you will waste time and get frustrated. Have a separate technical rehearsal.

Rehearse in front of a small audience weeks before your speech and listen to their comments attentively. Make it as real as you can – speak as if the real audience were present. Ask your audience to ask you questions, and to give you some feedback on your performance.

Time your speech over and over so it becomes a habit.

Manage your nerves by doing warm-up exercises – see Chapter 8 for some suggestions.

Appoint someone to film the entire rehearsal and play it back so you can learn from the process.

Appoint one person to take responsibility for running the rehearsal just as a director does in the theatre or a choreographer in the dance studio.

Get feedback on your delivery as well as on the content.

Attend to the temperature. Make sure your team is comfortable and alert.

Wear the clothing you are going to wear for the presentation at a full dress rehearsal and get feedback from someone you trust.

10

LEARNING THE LINES

Focus on the ideas you're trying to communicate –
ideas are easier to memorize than words.
Theresa Healey, actor

Do you struggle with learning or remembering your speeches?
If the answer is yes, then you're not alone. There are ways to
help you learn your content; you don't have to read your
speeches or rely on PowerPoint or notes to get through. The
key is to know and understand your key messages inside out
so even if your notes were lost or mislaid at the last minute
you could stand up and speak with utter conviction.

Find the meaning behind the words

We need to understand the meaning behind each paragraph,
thought or sentence before we can learn our lines. Understand
what you want to communicate, what it is you want to get
across, before even thinking about learning the material. This is
called the subtext of the communication. I always ask clients
briefly to summarize in a few sentences their messages before
they start writing their business presentations or speeches.

Constantin Stanislavski's bestseller, *An Actor's Handbook*, was one of my first acting textbooks. It is still my communication bible, which I use as a reference in business seminars and speeches. Stanislavski says, 'As soon as people, either actors or musicians, breathe life of their own into the subtext of a piece of writing to be conveyed to an audience, the spiritual well springs, the inner essence is released . . . The whole point of any such creation is the underlying subtext. If this were not the case, people would not go to the theatre but sit at home and read the play. We are inclined to forget that the printed play is not a finished piece of work until it is played on the stage by actors and brought to life by genuine human emotions.'

At the moment of performance the text is supplied by the playwright, and the subtext by the actor.
Constantin Stanislavski

Make your speech your own and then you will easily remember the material, especially if something goes wrong and the technology breaks down. Find a connection with the material and your emotions. Think of yourself as a storyteller having a conversation with your audience.

If you have written your own speech you are more likely to remember it because you are speaking in your own words. However, often speeches are written by others: public-relations consultants, freelance writers, press secretaries, journalists or even a talented friend happy to help out. Try to have some input into at least writing the structure of your speech before giving it to a writer to polish.

When I worked as a media officer for Helen Clark when

she was leader of the Opposition, I was always impressed that she wrote her own speeches and knew her material backwards. It showed every time when I observed her polished delivery.

Ask yourself every time you learn a speech: What do I mean here? What message do I want to convey? How can we learn the material if we don't understand its meaning? This is especially important if the material is technical. If you don't understand what you have written then it will be difficult to learn and deliver convincingly.

Stage fright

I have a recurring dream where I forget my lines on the stage in a play. I wake feeling humiliated and in a state of panic.

Stage fright is a very common fear when speaking in front of an audience or crowd of people. It doesn't matter if you work in business, the theatre, politics or education; we are human and sometimes we forget things.

The more we worry about this, the more we tend to lose our place. Sometimes in life we get what we think about. Instead of dwelling on the thought 'I will forget my words', try thinking 'I know my speech backwards'.

Trust in your memory. It will serve you and won't let you down if you have done your preparation and you are focused. Relax; the audience does not always know when you are panic-stricken or even lost for words. They may think you are pausing or creating suspense, or simply reflecting. I remember being mortified one night when I forgot my lines during the performance of a play.

I felt exposed and humiliated, and wanted to disappear on the spot. I spoke to friends after that opening night and they didn't even notice when I improvised to cover up the words I'd forgotten.

Be realistic: your memory will fail you at some stage. Be aware that it may happen. If you know your material well enough, you'll be able to think about the points you're trying to communicate, and pick up the flow again. After all, what's the worst thing that can happen? I wish I hadn't spent all those years worrying about forgetting my monologues – my ego was in the way and I was concerned about looking silly. If I'd just relaxed and trusted that I knew my material, my early days of public speaking and performing would have been a lot more enjoyable both for me and my audience.

Techniques for learning your lines

What did you do before exams at school to study your material? You became familiar with the material and understood it. There are many ways to learn material; we all learn in different ways. Apply your favourite techniques; for example at school I relied on visuals and imagery to learn. It doesn't matter what you do as long as the outcome is successful for you.

Key messages

What key messages do you want to communicate? If you had to summarize your speech in one sentence, what would it be? A 12-year-old must be able to understand your presentation.

Here's some jargon to remember. What's your Single Overriding Communication Objective – SOCO for short? What do you really want to say? In media training this jargon is used a lot to remind clients to know exactly what it is that they want to communicate. That one message must be worked out before you even begin to write your speech. If you cannot answer this, then the audience will never know what you are trying to communicate.

Take a large piece of paper or use the whiteboard and write

down your main ideas. Next, put them in an order of priority. I find it easier to memorize my messages in order so there is a logical sequence.

Understand the meaning behind each paragraph. 'Tell me in your own words,' I will often say to clients when speeches have been written for them by a speech writer. If you have to deliver the speech in one phrase, what would it sound and look like?

When you are familiar with your material, put your notes aside and rely on key bullet points to jog your memory. Lift your eyes off the page for long periods so they're not darting up and down like a yoyo. Never try to memorize your words and deliver them verbatim unless you are a trained actor.

Beginnings and endings

Do memorize the beginning and the ending of your speech. Learn these sections well so you feel secure – you don't necessarily need to know them word for word, but you need to have a clear idea of what you're going to say. The audience will particularly remember the beginning and the ending of your speech. Start by knowing exactly what you are going to say with conviction and confidence.

You can't make eye contact with your audience if you're looking at the page, at your notes or gazing at the carpet. Once we get through the first few minutes we typically feel more confident and start to relax. Knowing the beginning of your speech by heart will allow you to build an immediate rapport with the audience.

Use imagery

It helps to see images in your head – I often open a speech with a vivid story so I can engage the audience. This way I can easily remember the opening and it gives me time to settle in and relax. Stories are much easier to remember than lists of points. The best way to communicate is to say what you see in your mind. In other words, use your imagination to help you remember.

Think of yourself as a storyteller. You use anecdotes in many aspects of your life, especially if you are a parent. When we learn our material we are able to create magic for our audience because they get to experience our personality.

When I am coaching surgeons for their oral exams I ask them to see the operation in their minds as they answer the questions during a role play of an interview. This way they tell the story about what procedures they would use rather then just listing the facts from memory. This approach also prevents them delivering the answer in a monotone.

Write the words down
Another way to learn lines is to write the main points of the speech out again and again. This doesn't work for me but I know many for whom it does. I prefer to have a more spontaneous approach; my best speeches are usually well rehearsed so they appear spontaneous.

Say it aloud
Read your speech aloud on your own. Walk around the room at home, away from the busy work environment. Study and apply yourself in a relaxing environment or find some time in a quiet room to practise without any distractions.

Get a friend to help
Learn your material with a friend listening to you and prompting you. Your confidence will increase when you receive praise and feedback.

Record yourself
Film your speech. The more you play back your performance, the more you are able to sit back and hear the words, hear the subtext, and the speech as a whole. As a result you are having to absorb and assimilate the messages. This practice will help you feel more confident.

Mind mapping
Coloured pictures are helpful because you can easily memorize them and hold onto them in your mind. Mind mapping is a useful tool for remembering text. The more relaxed you are, the more you will assimilate. Many of my clients use this method to learn business material using coloured markers instead of the standard pen or pencil. See Chapter 6 for more information on mind mapping.

Learning environment
Give yourself the best possible environment in which to learn your speech. Some suggestions include:

- Play music that helps you to learn, unless you find it distracting.
- Turn off all phones, radios and televisions.
- Open a window to get some fresh air.
- Sit in a comfortable chair.
- Have healthy brain food such as nuts to nibble on. Never try to learn when you are hungry.
- Be alone when you are practising so you have no distractions. One of my more conscientious clients always puts aside some 'going over my speech time – no interruptions'. He is always very centred when he speaks to a large audience because he has put in the time required.

Equipment

I sometimes see speakers relying on PowerPoint to read the text of their speech, thinking they don't need to learn their material. This looks unprofessional and unconvincing.

Ask yourself why you are using this technology. If the answer is 'so I can read the words or feel secure with remembering my lines,' then you need to spend more time on your preparation and learn your material. It is off-putting and stilted to see speakers reading their notes with eyes down on the page or on the computer screen. It sends out a message to the audience, saying 'I don't think enough of you to learn my material,' resulting in a lack of connection with the audience. Appropriate use of PowerPoint in a presentation can be captivating if the speaker is confident but I prefer a presentation to involve the person without technology. It all depends on the audience, the purpose of the speech and the content.

Keep it in perspective

My niece Sarah is a lawyer and has always enjoyed public speaking. We chatted about her most memorable speech:

'One of the most significant public speeches that I presented was when I was at high school and I entered in a Maori speech competition. I spoke for 12–15 minutes in fluent Maori to a packed auditorium of approximately 2,000 people. It is traditional in Maori speeches not to use notes, therefore I presented the whole speech without notes and I also presented an impromptu speech in Maori after my main speech. Public speaking is difficult at the best of times, speaking publicly in a second language is even more of a challenge and it required weeks of preparation and rehearsing.'

I walked away from this conversation promising never to moan about learning material again. Sarah is part Tongan and has a passion for the Maori culture and language. When we want something badly enough we will remember our material because we will put the effort into our preparation.

TIPS ON LEARNING YOUR LINES

Read your speech out loud. This way you get to listen to your own voice and learn the content.

Learning the bullet points helps you to remember the structure and you can improvise around the key points.

Technology has its place. Many actors use dictaphones to memorize their lines.

Use colour. I find it useful to use coloured markers to emphasize key points in my notes.

Practise difficult words out loud. If you keep on fluffing a line when you rehearse, practise it out loud. Practise it as a tongue twister. Don't get hung up on it if you stumble.

Understand your content thoroughly so if you forget your lines, you'll be able to find different words.

Make it a priority to take time to learn your presentation.

Visualize the beginning and end of your presentation, and see a road map for how you intend to get there.

11

TRANSFORMING YOUR FEARS WITH SELF-BELIEF

Our deepest fear is not that we are inadequate. Our deepest
fear is that we are powerful beyond measure. It is our light,
not our darkness, that most frightens us. We ask ourselves,
who am I to be brilliant, gorgeous, talented and fabulous?
Actually, who are you not to be? You are a child of God.
Your playing small does not serve the world.
Nelson Mandela's Inaugural Speech, 1994

Many studies state that the most widely held fear is a fear of public speaking, even more common than a fear of death. Would most people really rather be in the coffin than give the eulogy?

Having had a fear about public speaking for many years, I can empathise with any of you reading this who are still declining speaking engagements. I now feel confident speaking in front of an audience and do so with passion and commitment. I embrace every opportunity to get my message across and make a difference to my listeners. You can do it too. If you've been asked to make a presentation, it's because someone believes in you and knows you can do it.

People often come up to me at the end of seminars and confess they've declined invitations to speak at functions because of terror. I say 'confess' because they tell me this with guilt and shame. There is no need to feel shame about being scared of speaking in public. You are brave every time you share your secrets about what you consider to be limitations. We all have fear in common. Most of us are afraid of something at some stage in our lives. You're halfway there by talking about these fears and sharing them with someone.

You can overcome your fears

Many clients who have come to see me have been reluctantly pushed, persuaded, or bribed because they can see that fear of public speaking is crippling their career opportunities.

We certainly aren't born with a fear of public speaking – it's a learned behaviour. Can you remember a time when you were told you were no good at speeches as a child, perhaps when you gave a morning talk or participated in a school debate? Were you laughed at, put down or discouraged from speaking again? Try to think about where your fear of public speaking may have stemmed from.

Even the experts feel afraid

We see actors, politicians, television presenters and celebrities on television and think their confidence at speaking in public comes naturally. However, even for experts, the nervousness doesn't go away.

We never think of experts such as professional actors being afraid of speaking in public. Actor Joel Tobeck says, 'I like the sense of freedom when I speak or perform in public. If the audience enjoys my performance, so do I . . . However, I still feel paralysed sometimes and ask myself, why am I doing this? Then the theatre takes over and you go on your professional instincts. As long as you trust yourself, you won't look a fool. It took me ages to learn this.'

Witi Ihimaera, who wrote the acclaimed novel *The Whale Rider*, also feels nervous before speaking in public. He says, 'My mother used to say, whenever I was anxious, "What's wrong with you? It's only fifteen minutes of the rest of your life." Whenever I face an audience and my knees start to tremble, I always think of that and it helps get me through.'

Within you right now is the power to do things you never dreamed possible. This power becomes available to you just as soon as you can change your beliefs.
Dr Maxwell Maltz

Fear of rejection

Do you relate to any of the following?

- I am afraid of failure in front of others.
- I am afraid of making a fool of myself.
- I am afraid of the audience laughing at me.
- I am afraid of getting it wrong.
- I am afraid of letting my company down.
- I am afraid of shaking.
- I am afraid of forgetting my words and my key messages.
- I am afraid of the first few minutes.
- I am afraid of blushing.

The list could go on for pages. All these phrases say the same thing: A fear of public speaking is actually a fear of rejection.

I must have spent at least half of my lifetime being afraid of rejection and taking criticism personally. I now learn from criticism but it has taken a lot of growing, maturity and education to be able to put my fears aside. All of us want to be liked.

What fear does to your body

Understanding how your body and mind react in times of stress will enable you to manage each situation. When we get stage fright and go blank in front of an audience it is because the stress chemicals are affecting our memories. I've had clients who tell me they are paralysed with fear when they deliver their speech. Many have felt faint and dizzy which is due to the interference with brain function caused by stress chemicals. Some have vomited before their speech. Often clients have arrived asking for painkillers for a throbbing headache because they are afraid of exposing their fears.

Fear distorts our perception and confuses us as to what is going on.
Dr Gerald Jampolsky, psychologist and author

When you are afraid, stress hormones are released into your body, resulting in a huge burst of energy that manifests itself as a pounding heart, intensified breathing, memory loss and sweaty palms. When we feel threatened, our flight or fight reflexes kick in and the body directs all the blood to the brain. British academic Bill Lucas says, 'The brain's efficiency can be reduced to as low as 10 per cent in pressure situations.' He suggests that plenty of water, a good diet, enough sleep, visualization and studying others can help.

Strategies for coping with fear

Do it anyway

When I started out as an actor I would sometimes decline television and film auditions because I was so terrified of failure. I would always regret it the next week. The day I got my first lead in a short film was the beginning of my accepting every audition. I knew I could do it – I would even call my agent before the audition to say, 'I'm going to get this role.' It took a lot of hard work and determination to get to this stage. You can make a decision to change and overcome your fears. No one can do it for you. You have to choose to do it.

> Nothing in life is to be feared. It is only to be understood.
> *Marie Curie*

Grab fear by the throat and shake it, tell it you are no longer afraid. Tell it to go away and that there is no longer a place for it in your life. Accept that you might always be at least a little frightened by public speaking – the fear might never go away completely. That burst of adrenaline before you start speaking is necessary to kickstart a great performance.

Prepare thoroughly

Most of us are nervous if we have never experienced something before or if we do not know what is going to happen.

> The day I don't get performance anxiety is the day I insult my audience.
> *Richard Burton, actor*

Professional speaker Lenny Laskowski says, 'Thorough preparation reduces your fear by 75 per cent'. In his experience, 'Proper breathing techniques can further reduce your fear by 15 per cent, and your mental state accounts for the remaining 10 per cent.'

A three-step approach

> Our greatest battles are with our own minds.
> *Jameson Frank*

Dr Gail Ratcliffe, a clinical psychologist who specializes in the diagnosis and management of stress, sees many clients with a phobia of public speaking. 'Some people come for help because they have a phobia of public speaking and it interferes with their working lives.' She has a three-part approach to managing fear, explained in detail in her book, *Take Control of Your Life*. In summary, the steps are:

* recognize what upsets you
* change the things you can
* change your attitude if you can't change the situation

Toastmasters

I often suggest to clients that they go to a local Toastmasters club to practise public speaking in a non-threatening environment. The Toastmasters organization has an excellent track record internationally, and is based on the principle of small groups of people meeting regularly to practise different types of presentations. Some of my clients have said they very rarely get the opportunity to speak in front of others, so when they do they feel rusty and frightened. Joining a public-speaking club is an excellent way to overcome these fears and to see you are not alone.

Ask for help

It's possible for you to overcome all of your fears with a little help from someone who's been there. A speaking coach or life-skills coach can be a great help.

> There are two types of speakers; those who are nervous and those who are liars.
> *Mark Twain*

Hundreds of people have signed up for three months of tuition, saying, 'I don't care how much this costs, I can't go on in my life feeling this afraid.' There comes a time with any phobia or limitation when you have to stop using fear as an excuse and take steps to overcome it instead.

Trust your audience

During my early business career I hated public speaking and only accepted invitations because it was a necessity professionally or rewarding financially. Working as the director of the Performing Arts School meant I had to be a spokesperson to media and speak at least once a month in front of a business audience, especially when I was seeking sponsorship. The bottom line was I was afraid of failure and looking foolish. In time my fears diminished. It was daunting for me at first speaking in front of business audiences. Gradually, my perception began to change. I started to realize they were just like me; they were human beings supportive of my messages. I was always amazed when someone would approach me and congratulate me on my speech.

It is your beliefs about the importance of what other people think about you that makes the difference. Fear of pubic speaking has more to do with fear of being negatively evaluated by other people than anything to do with the act itself.
Dr Gwendoline Smith, clinical psychologist

Change your habits

It takes between 21–28 days to change a habit according to Maxwell Maltz, author of *Psycho-Cybernetics*. We are often creatures of habit and changing our behaviour doesn't come easily. Think of all the fears you've overcome in your life. You need to apply the same principles to overcome your fear of public speaking.

I used to have a fear of drowning. I did almost drown in a public swimming pool when I was young and panicked. When I decided to conquer this fear by taking adult swimming lessons and learning to dive, my behaviour changed but it took real effort. What really made the difference was changing my thought process. I remember getting angry with the teacher and thinking, 'I'll show you I can dive!' To my amazement, I did.

Connect with your content

I asked a woman who came to see me about her fear of public speaking to tell me a travel story so I could get a sense of her communication style. To my surprise, she delivered a monologue with passion and confidence. She had no idea how captivating she was as a storyteller.

The challenge then was for her to channel this passion and

deliver an impromptu business speech with the same amount of energy. She was amazed to see her spontaneous perform- ance played back on film. She was expressive and natural. Most of my clients in this situation get to see that they are better than they think they are.

Trust yourself
Think of all your achievements in your life. What did you do to overcome your fear of heights or your fear of flying? What did you say to your child who was afraid of falling off his bike?

> What would you do if you knew that you could not fail?
> *Robert Schuller*

Think about when you've been frightened in the past. What happened? When? What sensations were going on in your body? How did you react? What mechanisms did you use to cope?

> I gain strength, courage and confidence by every experience in which I must stop and look fear in the face. . . I say to myself, I've lived through this and can take the next thing that comes along . . . We must do the things we think we cannot do.
> *Eleanor Roosevelt*

Learn from previous mistakes
The most successful people never let fear stop them from following their dreams. It is from mistakes and failures that we

grow. Without failure we do not learn. The greatest learning comes from that experience when everything went wrong.

The power of positive thought

What you think about is what you become. If you think you can, then you're right. If you think you can't, then you're also right.

According to life-skills coach Clive Littin, we have 30,000–40,000 thoughts a day! Let's use them to our advantage. How often do you have only positive thoughts before you speak in front of an audience or whilst sitting in a meeting?

It has taken years of practice for me to feel positive and excited before I speak but the odd negative thought can creep in so I repeat affirmations over and over to increase my confidence.

As a man thinketh in his heart, so is he.
Proverbs 23:7

My mother, Jean Eyre, is the most positive person I know. She grew up in the Second World War and had to leave school at 13 to help raise a family of eight children with her mother, a single parent. They were poor and lived in a modest house. She is always positive in her approach. I am grateful for this and so are my four brothers. She has taught me through her actions that you can be happy despite all the hardship and challenges in life.

According to the researcher at the Mayo Clinic in Rochester, Minnesota, 'being cheerful keeps you going.' The *New Zealand Herald* reported, 'In a study that spanned three decades, [it has been found that] optimistic people live about 19 per cent longer than pessimists.' 'It confirmed our commonsense belief,' said Toshihiko Maruta, a psychiatrist who was the lead researcher in the project. 'It tells us that mind and body are linked and that attitude has an impact on the final outcome, death.'

Analyse your thoughts.
His Holiness The Dalai Lama

Changing our state of mind is the beginning of changing our negative thoughts. I am rewarded every day in my work with positive feedback from once-terrified clients who jump through the fear hoop and come through it with more confidence. Conversations change from 'I can't do this' to 'I can do it!'

Affirmations

What is an affirmation? An affirmation is a strong, positive statement that something is ALREADY SO. Affirmations are based on the following principles:

- The outcome of your presentation will be a direct result of how you think about it.
- Change your thinking and the outcome of your presentation will change.
- Affirmations help you to change your thinking.

Of course, affirmations can be used in many different circumstances, not just in preparing for a presentation. I often use affirmations in all parts of my life.

Your personal beliefs have a major impact on your performance when you communicate with an audience. I was consumed with negative thoughts the weeks before most opening nights or live television shows. What if I fail? What if I'm not good enough? Why am I doing this? I could fill this page with the destructive dialogue that went on in my head.

Realizing I needed to find a way of being more constructive with my thinking I redefined my thoughts after observing successful friends who became my mentors and were living examples of how positive thinking could change a life. The more positive I was, the more successful I became.

Writing my affirmations down in a special notebook or speaking them aloud is useful. Sometimes I repeat one silently. Try to be specific. Here are some affirmations I use before I speak in front of any audience:

- I am a dynamic presenter.
- I am self-expressive.
- I communicate clearly and effectively.
- I am talented and creative.
- I love my audience and my audience loves me.
- I am confident and excited to share my knowledge.
- I am credible and professional.
- The more I know, the more I have to give my audience.
- I love my work and I am rewarded creatively every time I address an audience.

Turn the negative into a positive

> Actors commit so much to the work. It is so important to them, that acting always puts you in a life and death situation, and fear is a great energy.
> *Glenda Jackson*

Here are some comments from one of my public-speaking seminars organized by the Institute of International Research. The participants were asked to write down all their negative thoughts related to public speaking. They were then asked to replace these thoughts with constructive thoughts.

Negative	Positive
It's going to be a disaster	I'm well prepared
I'm going to make a fool of myself	I'm going to give the performance of my life
I'll forget my lines	I have learnt my speech well
Nerves will take over	I'm confident and in control
I'll be boring	I'm fascinating and will present with passion
I won't connect with the audience	I'm making eye contact
I feel hunched when I speak	I'm straight in my stance
I have negative body language	I'm expressive with my movements
I say too many ums	I'm a fluent speaker
I hate large groups of people	I'm at my best in front of groups
I don't know enough	I'm well prepared
I'm not a good speaker	I'm a fantastic speaker
They're not going to respect me	I'm well prepared and have earned their respect
I can't wait for it to be over	I'm going to enjoy it
I don't know where I'm looking	I'm looking at the audience
I'm so terrified of this experience	I can do this

Do you identify with any of these statements? Write down your negative thoughts about public speaking and consciously identify the positive alternative.

Visualize your performance

Let your imagination help you in your rehearsals for major speeches or presentations. When I'm rehearsing at home, I see the venue in my mind, see the audience, and imagine their response to my speech.

I have used this technique for most of my life; it helps to overcome fear and lets me plan for a successful outcome for my presentation. We use visualization every day, often without realizing it; we visualize the new home we want to buy, the new car we want or the healthy trim body we are exercising to achieve. When I was marketing the Performing Arts School, I would consciously visualize the new building I was looking for – it had to be large, have character, sound wooden floors, and so on. The perfect venue always turned up. I was positive and had high expectations that a more suitable building was always there for us. I would create a mental picture of what I wanted.

You can apply this approach to creating a successful outcome for your presentation. Experience your performance as though it is already happening. Have an open mind. We attract into our lives what we imagine most vividly. I always imagine my audience to be alert, focused, contented and motivated.

A simple visualization exercise

Get into a relaxed comfortable position, either sitting or lying down. Relax your entire body, closing your eyes. Now imagine yourself at the lectern or in front of your audience. You are speaking confidently, and know your material inside out. Your audience is responding with interest to you and your message. You competently handle any questions that arise. You finish your speech to warm and genuine applause from a smiling audience. A successful presentation!

Visualization and affirmation guidelines

- Phrase affirmations in the present tense, not in the future.
- Set your goal, such as mastering public speaking, or increased confidence when speaking.
- Create a picture. See yourself in front of a large or small audience, and think of it in the present tense as though it is happening now.
- Concentrate and focus on the idea. When you have accepted an invitation to speak to a group of people start to focus on it clearly throughout the day, so that it starts to feel like a reality.
- Make strong, positive statements. Think about yourself positively. See yourself as a dynamic communicator. See yourself receiving fantastic feedback and hear the applause.
- Have an open mind. Visualizing is not hocus-pocus; our sports champions have used it for years.
- Make your affirmations positive. Affirm what you do want, not what you don't want.
- The shorter and simpler the affirmation, the more effective it will be.
- Show your feelings. The more feeling your statement conveys, the stronger it is.

Stopping negative thoughts

Dr Gail Ratcliffe teaches many of her clients a simple technique called 'thought stopping'. In order to think positively, you have first to switch off the negative thoughts to allow room for the positive thoughts to take hold.

1. Select a thought that upsets you and which you have identified as being about a situation you cannot change.
2. Write down the thought you have chosen, and try to think of an alternative or replacement thought that you can live

with. For example, if you are feeling angry that your boss has asked you to speak at an upcoming corporate function, you could replace that thought with, 'Speaking at this function will be good for my career.' Keep the thoughts brief so they are easy to remember. The thoughts must be a true reflection of your feelings.

3. Write down your replacement thought, and accept it as your new attitude to this particular stressful situation.

4. Now, call up the old, upsetting thought into your mind. As soon as it starts to take shape, say STOP! Banish the thought and associated upsetting emotion from your mind. Next, say the replacement thought aloud and consciously introduce the positive emotion that is associated with this new thought.

Every day declare for yourself what you want in life. Declare it as though you have it!
Louise Hay

TIPS ON OVERCOMING FEAR AND BELIEVING IN YOURSELF

Write down your goals relating to improving your public speaking.

Stop all self-criticism.

Practise affirmations before every presentation.

Remember most of what you fear never happens.

Confide in someone regarding your fears about your public speaking. A problem shared is a problem halved.

Choose to be calm before speaking.

Never think of the audience as your enemy. They are on your side.

Decide to have fun when you next communicate in front of an audience.

Recall that speech that did work, hold onto that magical moment when the audience was right in the palm of your hand. Believe you can return to that place again.

Keep a brief record of all your successes when you speak, and refer to it when you are feeling nervous before a speech.

Ask yourself, is this presentation worth so much worry that my health is affected by it? The answer is no!

12

USING TECHNOLOGY
IN YOUR PRESENTATION

Technology on its own is not the answer –
it's what you do with it that counts.
Russell Hewitt, Managing Director, Vodafone Australia

Preparation for your presentation is everything. This particularly applies if you intend to use technology in your presentation, such as PowerPoint or a lapel microphone. There's nothing worse than seeing a speaker standing in front of an audience looking terrified because he doesn't know how to use the technology. You have to practise until you feel completely at home with the equipment you want to use.

Do I really need it?

The simplest speeches are often the most effective. If you want to use technology in your speech, ask yourself: does this technology help me to get my messages across or will it distract the audience? Be sure that you're not using technology because it's the modern thing to do, the boss has told you to, or just to make an impression. Technology is there to serve your audience, not to prop you up, or for you to hide behind or rely on in case you lose your way.

Technology is only an aid

Your ability to convey your message to your audience is all that matters. No amount of technology is going to overcome a lack of effervescence or content in your communication.

I'm not saying don't use technology; but please understand that only *you* can persuade, motivate and inspire your audience – the technology can't do this for you. You need to get the basics right first: passion and enthusiasm are more important than flashy technical skills. After all, you're there to share your message with the audience and to motivate them – if technology helps you to do this, great. But it should never be a substitute for delivering a well-rehearsed, passionate speech.

Are you a technophobe?

If you can see that technology would clearly add some value to your presentation, go for it. Don't let fear of technology be your excuse for not using technology at all. I was frightened of using technology in my presentations until patient support staff, friends and technicians over the years educated me how to use it properly.

Get some training and ask for help if you feel unsure. Your audience will be impressed if you are well prepared and show that you are at home with your equipment. Like everything that starts out being unfamiliar, the more you use specific technology the more you will understand its idiosyncrasies. And if it does let you down, carry on and display your magnif-icent public-speaking skills.

Keep learning about new equipment – try to stay up-to-date. You don't need to be a technical guru, but you do need to know what equipment is out there and how it might enhance your presentation.

Don't be a scrooge when it comes to technology. Inadequate out-of-date technology can hinder your performance. Invest in the best as it sends out a positive message that your company is techno-savvy and it says 'we mean business'. You don't need to purchase the equipment; the conference industry is well equipped to rent you what you need.

Technical rehearsals

Professional actors always have a technical rehearsal as part of their preparation for their performance. This rehearsal doesn't focus on the delivery of the words; it's about making sure the technology is working as it should. Apply this approach to your own speeches by making a point of trialing the technology before you speak.

It is a turn-off to watch someone from the audience fumble with PowerPoint or other equipment. I was absolutely terrified when I started presenting with technology and made more mistakes than I care to tell you. It becomes easy when you are familiar with any equipment; it simply takes time, practice and patience. It's only the unknown that makes you nervous.

Clients who schedule a technical rehearsal before a speech thank me afterwards for persuading them to make the time. Knowing in advance that your equipment is properly set up, and being comfortable with what you are going to say, are the keys to success.

Never make assumptions

If you are speaking at a function which you're not coordinating, don't assume the equipment you require will be available or compatible with your computer. Tell the organizers exactly what equipment you will need.

When I am asked to speak in a new place, I try to hire the same technology suppliers so I feel secure when I arrive. In this situation I always know that the equipment will be ready to go, and that a reliable technician will be available for the duration of my speech. This takes the stress away immediately.

Two London-based executive coaches I work with shared a story with me about the need to check and double check the technology infrastructure of speaking venues.

So annoyed were they with the five-star hotel they'd hired in central London that they sent this letter to the management over the technological hiccups they endured.

'The whole point of the meeting for which we hired your venue, and why we ran it as a buffet, was to run a 2.5 hours workshop based on a leadership DVD.

'We would have brought in our own portable player and even a large flat-screen TV if necessary, except they already had installed equipment available.

'Our DVD played on my machine at home and on my colleague's. It would not project on your screen when played.

'I was forced to leave the meeting and buy a new portable DVD from Selfridge's (around the corner) at a cost of £150. The DVD played on that but the image could still not be projected onto the large screen and they had no option for sound projection only from our equipment.

'In the end they were lucky to find us a 12 inch portable TV in the chef's room, to which we hooked up the new portable player.

'The chaos lasted for 90 minutes during which it was

impossible for us to conduct any kind of serious discussion with our clients; we had exactly one hour left to show them the DVD. We didn't run the workshop we planned at all.'

Have a back-up plan

Best-laid plans can go wrong. You need to be sufficiently comfortable with your material so, if your technology fails, you are ready to carry on regardless. For example, if you're using PowerPoint, have a complete handout document ready to distribute at the end of your speech; if your PowerPoint fails, your listeners will have the material to take away. If your computer battery fails, do you have your power cord as a back-up?

Audiences will understand; many will have had hiccups with technology themselves at some stage. It may even work to your advantage; you might become more engaging and spontaneous away from your visuals.

If the worst does happen, keep it simple. Stay calm, take a deep breath and you will find a solution. Make sure you practise the 'what if it breaks down' scenario in your rehearsal. Remember, if you have a technician present, then this is what he is paid to worry about, not you.

I remember a colleague recounting his near disaster when presenting a brand-development pitch to a client: he intended to take his laptop computer, overhead trans-parencies and a flipchart to the presentation. On arriving at the premises, he realized he'd left a vital connection for the laptop at his last presentation, in another city. The overhead projector's lamp had blown, and when he returned to his car to collect the flipcharts, he'd left the window down and rain had smudged the images! Luckily he'd arrived with enough time to redraw the two-colour logo before the meeting and he knew his material so well he didn't need to refer to the now-defunct PowerPoint presentation. He went on to win the contract.

PowerPoint presentations

Used correctly, PowerPoint can significantly enhance a presentation, especially if you're presenting facts and figures. It can provide clarity and impact; the golden rule is to keep it simple, colourful and legible. Judicious use of graphs can help your audience make sense of most financial information.

When writing a PowerPoint presentation, correct spelling and grammar are essential. Ask someone to proofread it for you. If you're using pictures in your presentation, make sure they are acceptable to your company. I remember a client getting into trouble with his employers because his pop-art visuals were deemed incompatible with the company's brand.

When using PowerPoint, the most common mistake is looking at the screen instead of maintaining eye contact with the audience. We've all been to presentations where speakers have used PowerPoint to mask their fear and a lack of knowledge of their material. Reading a PowerPoint presentation from beginning to end is a sure way to make your audience's eyes glaze over. Learn your material so you do not need to refer to the screen constantly.

I recall listening to three speakers who all used PowerPoint effectively in their presentations. They were Anita Roddick, talking about her business The Body Shop; Rob Hamill, Olympic rower, talking about his trans-Atlantic rowing adventure; and Peter Hillary on one of his trips to the Himalayas. What did these speeches have in common? The visuals did not get in the way and all speakers had a powerful story to tell, with or without technology. On all occasions, the visuals supported their speeches rather than led them.

Tips for using PowerPoint in your presentation

- Never read the presentation word for word off the screen; instead, have a short statement on the screen that you expand on in your speech.
- Keep it simple – no more than one idea per page.
- Less is best. Too much text on a slide takes the focus off you. My preference is no more than five words per sentence and no more than five sentences per page, and as few slides as you can get away with. Less than five is best.
- Use pictures or visuals to liven up the screen, but don't show too much detail – the audience won't be able to see it.
- Use contrast. A dark background works well with light lettering, and vice versa.
- Dream up exciting headings using adjectives. Be creative.
- If you are presenting overseas, make sure your software is compatible with the equipment at the other end.
- Don't forget your remote! Check it's packed before you leave the office.
- Be sure not to block the screen while you talk.
- Maintain eye contact with your audience throughout your speech.
- Don't overuse PowerPoint – it can turn your audience off and be the kiss of death for your presentation.
- You might also be able to hook up to the internet during your presentation – consider whether this is relevant to your presentation, or merely a distraction.
- Graphics for use in your PowerPoint presentation can also be sourced from the internet. Be aware of copyright law, however – you may need to ask permission.

How big should the screen be?

It is incredibly frustrating for the audience not be able to see the text clearly on a PowerPoint presentation. Technology company Sony recommends the following minimum screen sizes, depending on the number of people you are presenting to.

Audience Size	Screen Size	
	Feet	Metres
Up to 120	8	2.4
120–200	10	3.0
200–300	12	3.6
300–400	14	4.3
400–500	16	4.9
Over 500	20–25	6.1–7.6

Microphones

Consider whether you will need to amplify your voice using a microphone. Although you may prefer your natural voice, it can be tiring to have to speak loudly during a long presentation. Use of a microphone will depend on the size of the venue, the number of people you are presenting to and the acoustics of the venue. Find out whether your voice will echo when you are speaking; if the venue has lots of hard surfaces, this is a possibility.

There are three main types of microphone: fixed (usually attached to a lectern), hand held and lapel (usually attached to your clothing). Find out whether you will have a choice as to which type you use. If possible, use a lapel mike as this will give you freedom of movement.

Remember that microphones also pick up every sniff, cough and burp as well as your words. Don't get hung up about this, but be aware of turning off your mike or holding it well away from you if you want to blow your nose!

Rehearse with your microphone. Do a sound check with someone standing at the end of the room before your speech. If you're tall, be sure not to hunch over the microphone. Lastly, if you wear a lapel microphone, remember to turn it off when you leave the stage. The first time I worked with a lapel microphone, I discussed a member of the crew backstage while my microphone was still on; needless to say, he heard every word. I've never done it again.

I always say to clients that they should expect technology to break down, because it will. Don't worry about it – rather, go with the flow.

In September 2006 I was part of an audience in London listening to an invigorating lecture on communication. Two minutes into the start, the microphone went static and the speaker sounded like Donald Duck. We all cracked up laughing. Moreover, he had invited someone from the audience to contribute, but he sounded like Mickey Mouse. With our laughter drowning out Mickey and Donald, the faulty technology was abandoned and they projected their voices with power and clarity. Far from being a disaster, the technical failure actually broke the ice and created a more relaxed relationship between the speakers and their audience.

Microphone tips
- Allow enough time to check that the microphone is working and ensure a technician will be there to help if things go wrong. Have a contingency plan in case things don't go to plan.
- Find out how to turn the mike on and off.
- A microphone makes you louder, not more enthusiastic. You still have to put expression in your voice.

- Speak above the microphone, not into it. Hold the microphone just under your chin, not in front of your mouth.

DVD

Playing a DVD during your presentation is a winner if it is well presented and makes a point. We can get tired of listening to a speaker, especially during a long presentation, and a DVD can provide a change of mood. I've used DVDs with upbeat music or interviews with experts in a specific field to jazz up a presentation.

Sometimes you might have the opportunity to have a DVD made especially for your presentation. I once put together a short DVD showing what not to do when speaking in public. I performed in it – it was an effective way of showing what presentation mistakes look like, in a humorous and non-threatening way, and the audience responded warmly to the information.

If you're going to use technology to play comic cartoons, documentaries or anything visual, hire a large screen with good audio equipment. On many occasions I have sat in large rooms with big audiences where most people either couldn't see the small monitor or couldn't hear the audio due to poor sound quality. In such situations I frequently feel frustrated because I know that if the organizers had spent more money on their technology, the workshops would have been sensational. There is nothing worse than a serious endeavour degenerating into something resembling an amateur school production.

Presenting over the telephone

Speaking in business meetings using a conference phone can be a challenge; the audience you're presenting to isn't even in the room! Answer the telephone with enthusiasm and confidence; let your warmth come through. Sound professional and be clear with your diction. Organize the venue for the call beforehand so there are no distractions. When using the telephone, you really need to listen, as the audience's nonverbal cues won't be visible to you. You will have to gauge how your audience is feeling only by listening to their response.

> Is this the party to whom I am speaking?
> *Lily Tomlin,* More Power to You

The conference phone should not be used as a tool to vent anger or express upsets. Save important and confidential communication for when you are face to face.

Telephone tips
- Smile when you speak so you sound positive.
- Stand up or sit tall so your posture is correct and you feel confident and more energised.
- Be fully focused, don't be distracted, be in the moment.
- Go to a separate room if your environment is open plan.
- Greet the person as you would expect to be greeted.

Video conferencing
Pay attention to your body language when using video-conferencing equipment. Make sure your actions match your words. Remember to smile, be natural and project confidence. Avoid defensive body language and be energetic with your delivery – your audience can see if you're fidgeting or yawning. Treat the call as a performance. Use short, simple, succinct sentences and limit the number of participants if possible. Sit

in a comfortable chair (poor posture affects your voice) and use notes if you need them.

> Suit the action to the word, and the word to the action.
> *Hamlet, William Shakespeare*

Mobile phones/PDSs

They have taken over our lives; I cannot imagine my life without my iPhone. I used to enjoy the leisurely Heathrow Express train journey to the airport and listen to classical music on my iPod; now I spend the entire time talking to my business partner and managing my social life.

Make sure you turn your phone off before you make a speech or go into a meeting. My golden rule is to turn it off the moment I arrive at the venue – it's very easy to get distracted and forget such a simple thing. It's inevitable that someone in the audience will forget to turn off their mobile so it's worth asking the person introducing you to remind the audience before you begin speaking. And it goes without saying – if you're in the audience, make sure your phone is turned off, or if it's an emergency, switch it to vibrate only. It's so disrespectful to speakers to have a mobile ring during the presentation, and it can really affect their concentration.

In 2005, at the request of Nick Batchelor, managing director of Telecom UK and Europe, I led a two-day presentation workshop at Foxhills, a beautiful country estate outside of London. At the start of each day he asked me to take every mobile phone from his team. The participants were not in the least bit offended. (Of course, they received their

BlackBerrys back at the end of the day.) This will now be standard procedure, and I recommend that every trainer does likewise.

TIPS ON USING TECHNOLOGY EFFECTIVELY

Ask yourself if it's necessary to use technology in your speech – it won't be appropriate for all types of speaking engagements.

Make sure you know how to use the technology if you do decide to use it.

Have a back-up plan in case it doesn't work. Be prepared for a disaster, and arrive early enough to put your back-up plan into action if it's needed.

Don't expect the technology to help you to be a dynamic and convincing speaker; these attributes have to come from you.

Set your technology up before your audience arrives; I've seen speakers spend five minutes mucking around with equipment while the audience waits. It looks unprofessional and disorganized.

Technology is there to enhance your communication, not to replace you.

13

SETTING THE STAGE

All the world's a stage
And all the men and women merely players.
William Shakespeare, As You Like It

The place where you deliver your presentation plays a big part in determining whether your speech will be successful. Your audience will be more open to your messages if you are all at ease in the environment. If at all possible, become as familiar as you can with the room in which you'll be delivering your speech.

If you work in a pleasant environment you'll appreciate how surroundings can affect your morale; it's the same for your audience. Lighting, air conditioning, room size, decor and sound quality all play an important part in our ability to retain information. We want our audience to enjoy listening to us and to remember our speech. This means taking the time to create an atmosphere which will allow this to occur – every detail counts.

It's not essential to hold your speech in an up-market hotel, although this can work well if it suits your content and audience. Think about what type of venue would reinforce the messages you want your audience to remember. What type of venue would help to establish your credibility as a speaker? What kind of impression do you want to make?

I recall turning down a training job because the venue was on the *Spirit of Adventure*, a well-known sailing ship. My tendency towards seasickness meant that it wouldn't have been a successful presentation. Know your limits – it's fine to stay inside your comfort zone.

Of course, venues can change at the last minute. I saw this happen with a team of people who had been rehearsing with me for a number of days. When we turned up for the dress rehearsal, we were informed the presentation was actually to be held on a luxury launch. We had no time for an onsite rehearsal, but we were able to get there early enough to see the stage and make decisions about where the screen was to be placed. If you're familiar with the important points of setting up a room, you'll know what to focus on if your preparation time is cut short.

Venue organizers aren't mind readers

Always provide your venue organizer or conference logistics manager with a comprehensive brief, setting out your requirements. Fax or email clear instructions about the size of the room, equipment required, projected start times and breaks, food and beverage requirements and all ancillary equipment. Then double check by phone to see if those instructions have arrived. Make no assumptions. Are there any special needs, like wheelchair access for a disabled member of the audience?

Get a name! Should you need to go over the instructions again, it helps to know who you spoke with last time.

Ask questions

You or your support staff should ask the appropriate person as many questions as you can think of. This may seem obvious, but if you run through the checklist later in this chapter, you have a good chance of uncovering any hiccups before D-day. Check and double check that the arrangements are to your satisfaction.

I have often arrived in another city to discover there has been a mix-up with the room, due to a breakdown in communication. I remember arriving on the morning of one presentation and discovering that my seminar room didn't have a door. This was not satisfactory, especially because the French rugby team was touring at the time, so the outside noise from the players, their entourage and the press was very distracting. Had I asked whether the room could be shut off from the rest of the hotel before arriving at the presentation, it would have saved the last-minute rush to find a more suitable venue within the hotel.

On another occasion, I assumed that the organizers of a function I was speaking at would have made a hotel reservation for me as the presentation was out of town. Unfortunately the hotel had made the reservation for the following night instead, and as luck would have it, all other hotels in the city were full. I didn't fancy sleeping on a park bench! It was sorted out eventually, but it made my preparation for the speech more stressful than it needed to be.

Covering all bases

Personally, I prefer to undertake the final series of checks myself. Always allow enough time to make alterations to the room if for some reason it does not meet your expectations. There are usually a couple of last-minute things to organize, no matter how thoroughly you've prepared.

I always inspect the venue the evening before my presentation, which necessitates an overnight stay if the job is out of town. I remember co-facilitating a two-day presentation-skills course, when my co-presenter hadn't arrived by the starting time. Her aircraft had been diverted because of bad weather, and our presentation was delayed by an hour. If your speaking engagement is out of town, plan to arrive the day before if possible to avoid stressing yourself out.

What do you need to check?

A welcoming environment

Would you want to spend time in the designated room if you were a member of the audience? Does the room need fresh flowers? A good tidy-up? Some welcoming touches such as a person to show people to their seats? Classical music or some soothing, feel-good jazz?

Think about whether the environment reflects your business brand. Do the furnishings send out an appropriate message? Presenting in a shabby room will distract from your credibility no matter how strong your message.

See the room at least a day before your presentation. If you need to dress the set, then do it. Tell your organizers and technical crew where you need everything or set it up yourself.

Lighting

If you have the choice, deliver your presentation in natural light. Fluorescent light can be a strain on your eyes and sometimes makes a buzzing noise, making the speaker difficult to hear. If you don't have a choice about presenting under fluorescent lights, be empathetic with tired audiences and make allowances for breaks if necessary.

Check if any of the light bulbs in the room need replacing.

I recall helping a client with his speech in a boardroom with a faulty flickering light. It was so distracting, we decided to continue working with the lights off – there was enough natural light to see, I hasten to add.

Consider whether you need specific lighting focused on you. For example, if you're presenting in a darkened room with a notebook computer, its screen may give your face a spooky glow. Fortunately, many projectors are bright enough to allow you to keep some lights on, which is vital for eye contact. If you need to turn the room lights off to achieve a bright image on the screen, it might be time for a new projector or data show.

A spotlight directly overhead can cast a shadow under your brow. For major presentations, a pair of spotlights (one either side, tilting down at 45 degrees) will make you look friendly and approachable. If you're going to move around the stage, you'll need a 'stage wash', which lights the entire stage.

You can hire a lighting technician to advise on appropriate lighting and to provide the necessary equipment – don't feel you have to arrange it all yourself.

Temperature
Temperature is critical to the success of your presentation. There is nothing worse than sitting through a speech when you are sweltering hot or freezing cold. Check the temperature one hour before the audience arrives, and communicate any concerns to the staff.

Air-conditioning is not easy to get right but the last thing you need your audience to do is to doze off because it's hot and stuffy. A large audience will warm up the room, so it's better for it to be on the cool side to start with. Somebody in your audience will always let the organizers know if it's too cold. Think carefully about your clothing so you don't get too hot while presenting.

Air quality can be improved by including plants in the room; the more the better but even six can make a difference. And it goes without saying: never allow smoking in a room while you are speaking.

Seating

We expect our audience to sit and listen to us – the least we can do is make sure the seats are comfortable and that the audience can actually see us from where they are sitting. Thankfully, most hotels and conference centres have made a substantial investment in comfortable furniture.

Ask the staff to remove empty chairs before you start speaking, if this can be done discreetly. Empty chairs remind you and your audience you were expecting more people than have shown up.

Consider the level of audience interaction you would like when choosing your seating arrangement. Usually I like to encourage as much audience participation as possible by removing tables and sitting people in a circle. You don't always have a choice if you are giving a presentation around a client's boardroom table; if this is important, you may like to invite the client to your premises instead.

The size of your audience will determine which seating arrangement you choose. If you're using screens or tables, think about where you want them to go. I prefer a U-shape for audiences of 25 or fewer, where the seats are arranged in a large circle with a small gap for me at the top. This allows me to maintain eye contact with everyone. Circles and semicircles work because they feel inclusive and informal. For a larger group my preference is a classroom style. Of course, you may not have an option; the majority of my speeches are on a platform with a microphone to a larger audience of 100 or more, where theatre-style seating is the only practical seating arrangement.

Seating arrangements
Semi-circle/U-shape
For up to ten people, this seating arrangement allows you to have eye contact with everyone in the group and, because it feels intimate, your audience will be more inclined to ask questions and participate. I prefer not to have a table between me and the audience if possible. If you are presenting at a brainstorming session, a full circle may feel more appropriate.

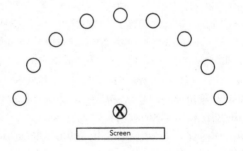

Boardroom

A presentation to a small group around a boardroom table can be useful if your audience needs a surface to write on, or if coffee and tea are served during the presentation. Props like flip charts can be useful in this instance. The audience should not sit on the same side of the table as the speaker.

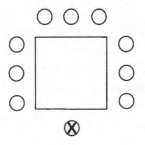

Theatre style

If you're presenting to a large number of people, theatre-style seating is probably the only option you'll have. Remember to place the chairs so each person is looking between the two people in front rather than at the back of someone's head. It can be useful to avoid arranging the seating with a centre aisle if you think you'll be distracted by the gap in the middle of the room.

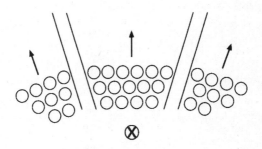

Technology

If you are relying on the venue organizer to provide computer equipment, make sure you have a run-through before the day of the event.

I have often sat in an audience feeling frustrated for the speaker because the laptop has been set up on the wrong table or on the wrong side of the room. I recall one CEO who constantly turned his head to the screen behind him, instead of referring to the bullet points on the laptop's display in front of him. Many years ago in the good old days of overhead projectors, a client asked me to stop moving my head every time I changed an overhead transparency because it was so distracting – I never did it again.

Your microphone is an important piece of technology – even if you prefer not to use one, it may pay to have one available just in case you find yourself competing with a road drill or a noisy digger outside while speaking.

Music

Well-chosen music builds atmosphere prior to an event or conference, but you must pick the right music for the event. Consider your audience and your subject material when deciding what type of music would be appropriate. Ask other people for their opinion about your music selection. Instrumental music is a safer choice as music with lyrics runs the risk of distracting your audience.

Most hotels have an excellent selection of music CDs available for use. If you have clear requirements or set ideas, make sure you communicate this to your contact person at the venue.

Fading the music tells your audience that the presentation is going to start.

Handouts and props

You may like to provide the venue with a copy of any handouts you are planning to distribute at the end of your speech, in case you accidentally leave them behind at the last minute. If you are presenting at a conference, there will probably be a date by which you have to provide all your handout materials to the conference organizer.

Leave yourself enough time to double-check that you have any props you need for your presentation. Don't let it happen to you. But sometimes even when you have been meticulous in your organization, some things are out of your control and accidents do happen.

In my case, the handouts were copies of my book which I needed to have at my first ever public presentation in the UK to a group of 120 business people on the penthouse floor of a London office building.

But the courier company managed to lose boxes – boxes of the copies which probably totalled around 300. Instead of being expertly displayed on a table in that penthouse ready for me to sign and present to the audience, they were sitting in some depot, somewhere, that someone can't explain to me to this day!

Although gutted and upset there was nothing I could do, so I opted instead to focus on how something good comes out of upset if you accept the situation.

I weaved the story into my presentation, casting myself as the author who'd lost her books. Ironically, because I wasn't behind a table signing copies at the end of the event, rather mingling and networking with people, I formed a lot more business relationships that night than I otherwise would have.

If my story has any meaning, it's that over-dependency on your handouts and your props puts you at risk of freaking out if something goes wrong. When it does, turn down the drama and turn up the calm crisis management. Sometimes things just happen for a reason.

Overseas engagements

When I travel to give a speech, I always carry everything I might need for the performance in my cabin luggage. I was caught out once when I arrived at my destination – minus my luggage. I had to go out and buy an entire outfit in an hour – using up valuable time when I should have been focusing on my upcoming speech.

A client had a similar experience, where everything she needed was in her cabin luggage – except her shoes. When her bags failed to arrive in Washington DC, she had to go shoe shopping, instead of using the rehearsal time to prepare for the speech.

Your venue checklist

• Where is the venue?
• Who is responsible for setting up the room?
• What are their contact details?
• Will they be in the room while you are speaking?
• What date and time is the speech?
• What time will the audience start arriving?
• Where will the audience gather before the presentation?
• Is your accommodation booked (if out of town)?
• How are you getting to the venue?
    airfares
    taxi
    if using your own car, is there parking?
• What equipment will you be bringing yourself?
    laptop computer
    hand-outs
    music

computer disc with your presentation
hard copy of speech
- What equipment do you need the venue to provide?
  data show
  laptop computer
  DVD player
  screen
  microphone
  lectern
  music
  CD player or tape recorder
  sound system
  electronic board
  whiteboard
  flip chart paper
  coloured pens (that work)
  pads and pencils (at back of room or on seats)
- What technical support do you need?
  lighting technician
  sound engineer
  will they be available for a rehearsal?
- What room will you be speaking in?
  how big is it?
  what is the seating arrangement?
  can the audience see you from any seat?
  will any plants/flowers be provided?
  can the room be darkened if necessary?
  how is the room's air-conditioning controlled?
  is there sufficient natural light?
  where are the power connections?
  where will the AV equipment be set up?
  what are the acoustics like?
  will you need a microphone for people at the back of the

room to hear you?

can you hear noise from other conference rooms in the building from inside your room?

is there adequate access for disabled members of the audience?

• Will food and drink be provided as part of the function?

are there any special dietary requirements?

will there be a glass of water for you during the speech?

is there water for the audience?

what time will the breaks be, if any?

where are the bathrooms?

TIPS ON SETTING UP THE ROOM

Communicate what you need to your conference organizers. They're not mind readers.

Arrive early enough to do something about it if it's not right.

Have a microphone check, including checking the height so you are speaking across it, not hunching into it or over it.

Will you have your notes in your hands or on the lectern? Don't forget your reading glasses, if you need them.

Have a bathroom visit and check your image, hair, make-up, tie, etc, before starting the presentation.

Make sure you have a glass of water handy in case you need it.

Turn off your mobile phone.

Can everyone see you in the room? Is the seating suitable?

Try to have no physical barriers, such as tables between you and the audience. Don't hide behind a lectern.

Announce break times at the beginning of your presentation, and have a break at least once every 90 minutes.

Be clear and firm about how you would like the room to be set up – it's your presentation.

14

HEALTH AND WELLBEING

For fast acting relief, try slowing down.
Lily Tomlin, Actress

How does your health impact on your public-speaking ability? Your health impacts on every area of your life. When you're in top shape, you can use your energy to make your presentation sparkle.

Sometimes poor health is a short-term occurrence, such as when we're exhausted after a sleepless night, or have jet lag or even a shocking hangover. I have often given a speech on a few hours sleep because the hotel I was staying in was noisy. The challenge is to become energized and focused before delivering the speech.

Longer-term health issues take more work to clear up, but I encourage you to address any problems you may have in order to focus properly on your presentation. If your health issues are outside your control, still take responsibility for living as healthily as possible in order to manage your condition successfully.

Managing stress

Your personal life impacts on your professional life.

Only intimacy with the self will bring about healing.
Deepak Chopra

You cannot give a lively, convincing speech if you feel as if your personal life is out of control. I often communicate with human-resource managers to request time off for a client facing burnout, and to set up support structures within companies to help people realize they must rest and take responsibility for their health. When people are at the point of exhaustion they are sometimes unable to recognize the signs of extreme stress or burnout.

Burnout Test

Clive Littin, personal and business coach, has the following test for assessing how close you are to burnout. Score yourself from 0 to 5 for each question, with 0 being a definite no and 5 being a definite yes.

1. Do you tire easily?
2. Is joy elusive in your life?
3. Do your friends say, 'You don't look well'?
4. Are you becoming increasingly cynical, negative, disenchanted?
5. Are you invaded by a sadness you can't explain?
6. Are you forgetting things like appointments and deadlines?
7. Are you increasingly irritable, short-tempered, disappointed in the people around you?

8. Are you too busy to do even routine things like making your bed, phone calls, sending Christmas cards?

9. Are you seeing close friends and family less often?

10. Are you suffering from aches, pains, headaches, a lingering cold?

11. Do you feel restless, disoriented when your day is over?

12. Do you have little to say?

13. Is sex more trouble than it's worth?

14. Are you unable to laugh at a joke about yourself?

15. Do you seem to be working harder and getting less done?

Score

15–25   You're fine

26–35   Watch out

36–50   You're a burnout candidate

51–65   Burnout

65+   You're in danger

We all need some stress to perform – it gets the adrenaline going. However, stress levels become unhealthy when they are out of control.

> So few of us know how to relax. We have come to believe it is necessary to go at 100 per cent all of the time.
> *Sven Hansen, Salus Executive Health*

When I make a speech in the middle of the day I organize my schedule around it so I am relaxed and focused. I always go home, shower and change if I have a major presentation after work so I feel fresh. Sometimes I make a note in my diary to go for a short walk several hours before my speech.

It's well known that stress contributes to any illness and increases the symptoms. Being fully prepared before a presentation will help to reduce stress. Increased blood pressure will not help you when you need to feel calm and in control in front of an audience.

Dr Susan Gee, research fellow at Victoria University's School of Psychology, says, 'The way an individual handles a potential crisis plays a part [in stress management]. One person might see stress as a challenge, but someone else may say, "It's too much, I can't deal with that."' Choose not to let the stress of your presentation affect your life. Chapter 11 discusses changing beliefs and using visualization and affirmation to create positive thoughts about public speaking.

My personal philosophy is to try not to view a crisis or stress experience as something bad. Instead, I try to see it as healthy change or transition. All your experiences are valuable material for your presentations and are nothing to be ashamed of. I have more to contribute because of my failures and weaknesses. Ask yourself – why am I finding this situation stressful, and what strategies can I put in place to ensure it doesn't happen again?

Medication

If you are prescribed medication for anxiety and stress, work with your doctor so you are monitored, and ask if there are perhaps some more holistic ways to overcome this problem. One client became so addicted to relaxant drugs she felt she couldn't give a presentation without them. It was her goal to present without medication. She now speaks in front of large audiences drug free. We worked together on her fears and followed a more holistic path.

Headaches

Have you ever had a headache before speaking in public? According to Annemarie Colbin, author of *Food and Healing*, headaches are caused by:

a) expansion of the blood vessels in the head (vascular headaches); or
b) tension or strain in the muscles in the neck, scalp, or face (tension headaches).

She goes on to say that vascular or 'expansion' headaches are usually the result of:

• too much liquid of any kind, including fruit juice
• alcohol
• ice cream and other cold and highly sugared foods.

Tension or 'contraction' headaches are usually the result of:

• tension and overwork
• heat
• meats and salty foods (especially on an empty stomach)
• lack of food and/or fluids
• excess mental concentration or physical activity in addition to the above.

If you have a headache, consider whether any of the above could be the underlying cause, and put strategies in place to prevent the situation from happening again.

The reducing stress commandments

I have carried around different versions of these reducing stress commandments and put them on the fridge to remind me of what I need to do in the weeks leading up to an important speech. I have no idea who wrote them, but they seem to apply well to public speaking.

Ten commandments for reducing stress
  1. Thou shalt not be perfect nor even try to be.
  2. Thou shalt not try to be all things to all people.
  3. Thou shalt leave things undone that ought to be undone.
  4. Thou shalt not spread thyself too thin.
  5. Thou shalt learn to say 'No'.
  6. Thou shalt schedule time for thyself, and thy supportive network.
  7. Thou shalt switch off, and do nothing regularly.
  8. Thou shalt be boring, untidy, inelegant and unattractive at times.
  9. Thou shalt not even feel guilty.
  10. Especially, thou shalt not be thine own worst enemy, but be thy best friend.

Look for balance

Finding time to do all the things you want to do is tough. When one area of your life starts to affect the quality of other areas, it might be time to do some rebalancing of priorities. Often, when life gets too frantic, health is one area that starts to suffer, because we don't place enough importance on it until we don't have it any more. Achieving a balanced life takes planning and commitment – simply saying 'I should work less and exercise more' won't work unless you put a plan in place to achieve your goal.

Psychologist Hank van Bilsen says, 'The best protection is a balanced lifestyle.' He suggests a 'reasonably pleasant job' that you don't invest too many hours in, good friends, interests in sports, academic and spiritual things and enjoying being on your own.

One of my best friends died in her early thirties from breast cancer. She worked in a demanding profession enduring long hours and was also a solo parent. She was always telling me how she wanted to cut down her hours and enjoy life more. Her death woke me up and made me look at my workaholic habits. It made me see that I wasn't having enough fun or setting aside relaxation time. She knew she'd a lump in her breast for years but ignored it for a long time. She hated her job but continued with it. Her death made me realize only I could make myself set aside time to relax and do the things I really wanted to do away from work. Life is not a dress rehearsal.

Medical conditions

Performing requires you to be alert and focused, and to look lively and well. I was diagnosed with endometriosis in my early twenties. I had never heard of it – I couldn't even pronounce the word. Many of you reading this chapter will perhaps have a secret medical condition that no one knows about in your workplace. Many years of presenting before an audience when I was ill has taught me to manage my health and my life so I can continue to perform effectively. I initially chose not to discuss my condition with anyone apart from family and friends. However, I revealed the information in one media interview, which changed my mind about speaking out in the workplace and sharing my story in speeches, especially to women.

When I was very ill with the disease, the audience never knew otherwise. I have my acting career to thank for that. I often collapsed when I got home, wondering how I was ever going to get out of bed the next day and perform. I have studied nutrition, relaxation techniques, neuro-linguistic programming and other helpful techniques, which have taught me to manage my health carefully. My personal circumstances influenced me to include this chapter in this book.

I recommend reading *It's a Great Life When You're Well* by Eileen Evans, registered naturopath. She is a great example of what happens when you live a well-balanced life. In her sixties she stills glows with good health. In 1997 she was presented with a lifetime-achievement award from the natural health industry for dedication to public education. I have relied on medical drugs off and on for many years now and am grateful for their existence but I also try to lead a carefully managed life with strict regimes around food. There is a place for prescription drugs, but I highly recommend a straight-forward natural-health management plan to build your immune system and get you onto a more natural road.

Strategies for coping with illness
Dale was diagnosed with leukaemia in 2001. She chooses to retain her high-profile job, while battling her illness with chemotherapy. I admire her attitude, which has always been positive. She speaks in public and chairs meetings regularly. Her strategies for dealing with her illness are to 'schedule my meetings accordingly, take naps, splash water on my face or take a walk.' She advises those living with illness 'not to be hung up on whether you are going to live or die. Get rid of all negativity, including negative people in your life. Get rid of things in your house you do not want. Everyone manages things differently – do what works for you.'

Food and body image
So many clients complain about their weight when they see the film of their presentation rehearsals. Focusing on your weight gets in the way of a successful presentation and affects

your confidence. We need to learn to feel comfortable with our own bodies. Accept your body type or do something about it.

It's not about dieting – it's about changing your life.
Oprah Winfrey

Working with a client who lost over three stone during the course of a year was an inspiring experience. When I was first introduced to her she was quite large and had very little self-esteem. She decided to embark on a confidence-building journey, losing weight and overcoming her fear of speaking in public. As a result, her life has taken off! When we started working together she wore baggy clothes which were two sizes too big. She now looks elegant, attractive and professional.

I recall sitting in on a workshop where the lead facilitator was extremely overweight. Some days later, someone who had been in the audience said to me, 'Why should I listen to anyone carrying that much weight?' I was dumbfounded. The speaker's workshop hadn't gone well and I was trying to figure out why. Unfair as it may seem, this person didn't look professional and well groomed in the eyes of the audience. Many politicians and public figures have made an effort to shed excess weight and as a result have gained respect and popularity.

Healthy eating
Working with clients to develop a nutritious eating plan has become an important part of my work. I am amazed at the number of people who tell me they don't eat regular meals

throughout the day. It is not unusual for me to hear people say 'I'm too busy to eat.' I used to be one of those busy people who went five hours without food or water and wondered why I was shaking every time I made a speech or led a training session.

Eat lightly, and every three hours, to keep your sugar levels even and always have breakfast before a major presentation. Eating well and often has changed my life. I have more energy because I monitor my eating habits. I now eat for fuel.

Breakfast – eat it!

For many years, I lived on coffee for breakfast. I had to learn the hard way not to skip the most important meal of the day. Your body needs looking after, and eating breakfast, particularly when you are about to give a speech or run an important meeting, is crucial. Eat breakfast even if you aren't hungry. You need the energy to keep you going.

I have seen many chief executives over the years catching early planes, eating high-fat processed plane food and drinking six cups of coffee a day. It's the easy solution, but it's not healthy. When I need to be on an early flight, I wake at 5.30 a.m. and eat my standard gluten-free muesli, yogurt and fruit before the taxi arrives. I now arrive for my first meeting feeling lighter and more energetic.

Alcohol

Never drink alcohol before speaking in public; even a glass can result in you slurring or prevent you from performing to your best ability.

Eileen Evans says that alcohol can, both directly and indirectly, cause many illnesses which have been associated with nutritional deficiencies. She goes on to say that experimental studies have shown that 81 per cent of chronic alcoholics, when treated with a well-balanced diet plus supplements, were still sober after six months. Only 38 per cent of alcoholics were still sober after six months when treated with a standard hospital diet.

Over the years I have worked with many clients who struggle with their high alcohol consumption. They continue to deliver and perform well in their business roles but their livers are unwell and they feel fatigued most of the time.

If you do drink alcohol, drink extra water to keep yourself hydrated. Have a few alcohol-free nights per week and remember that alcohol is a depressant so if you have a speech coming up refrain from drinking the night before. Plan to abstain completely from drinking for at least a week each month.

Keep a diary for six months
Start observing and writing down everything you eat. This sounds obsessive but it is one way to help clean up your life. Bill McKay, a strict naturopath, gave me this exercise to kickstart the new millennium in January 2000. I kept a record for a year and eventually realized the link between the type of food I was eating and my energy levels. I am so grateful to him for helping me to become aware of what I am eating.

Exercise
Exercise is absolutely essential to your mental and physical wellbeing. Find an aerobic activity you love and do it regularly. Thirty minutes of reasonably vigorous exercise four to five times a week will reward you with lower stress levels, a healthier heart, better sleep, more stamina,

improved concentration levels . . . the list goes on. You simply can't afford not to make exercise a priority in your life.

Those who think that they have no time for bodily exercise will sooner or later have to find time for illness.
The Earl of Derby, quoted in Take Control of Your Life

If you are starting to exercise for the first time, or if it's been some time since you last exercised, take it slowly. Focus on developing an exercise habit you'll be able to maintain, rather than pushing yourself too hard and then giving up.

Relaxation

Recharging at health hideaways has become an important part of my 'wellbeing' regime. When I return from time spent at a health retreat, I am calmer, fitter, happier and ready to get back into my work with more energy. I feel energized after eating only 'clean food' (no meat, salt, dairy, preservatives, coffee, tea or wine) and doing regular exercise.

Attending a health spa is something I do as a result of making a decision to have better strategies in place to manage my health. I realized I was not always as disciplined about looking after my needs as I thought I was. My promise to myself now is to attend a health retreat at least once a year for the rest of my days. I realize the importance of rest and rejuvenation for my productivity and creativity as well as my health and peace of mind. I am of no use to my friends, clients or audience when I am stressed.

You can also implement strategies in your daily life to help you relax and prepare for the day ahead. One friend chooses to rise at 5.00 a.m. to meditate before her children and husband wake up. She has a demanding corporate role and finds that meditation helps her to be calm and ready for the day.

There are many forms of relaxation practices – find one that suits you and incorporate it into your daily life. Investigate yoga, pilates, Tai Chi, the Feldenkrais method, the Alexander Technique, holistic massage or Hellerwork.

When I am tutoring one on one I will often get the client to participate in a theatre-based improvisation exercise with me to relax the body and mind. Inevitably they will end up laughing because they feel silly. What makes you laugh? Who makes you laugh? I realize I have surrounded myself with people in my life who lighten me up when I get too serious and worried about giving a speech. Call a friend or colleague who makes you laugh if you feel yourself getting stressed before a presentation. Laughter exercises your throat, stomach, face and diaphragm, stabilizes your blood pressure and strengthens your immune system. It also releases tension and stress.

Connect with nature

Nature heals you and makes you feel better about life. Take a walk before you speak even if it's just for five minutes. Walk to the venue or have a power walk that morning in a park or on a beach. Walking in the fresh air gets your problems into perspective. For years I have been walking near the sea and alongside a marina where I gaze at boats and watch the sun go down. My exercise clothing is always in my bag when I am out of town for a speaking assignment.

Ask for help

Enlist support when you need it. People will say no if they can't support you. People often refuse to ask for help because they fear rejection, don't want to be seen as weak or a burden, or simply feel they should be able to carry on without support. Get rid of all the 'shoulds' in your language. Some of the best speeches I have given have been as a result of asking for help.

TIPS ON MANAGING YOUR HEALTH

Drink water or a soothing calming herbal tea before you speak. Avoid coffee prior to any major presentation, as caffeine will make you more nervous. Also, avoid drinking alcohol before any presentation, even if you are the after-dinner speaker. Alcohol affects your attention span, memory and speech.

Always have filtered water with you when you speak and sip it when your mouth feels dry. Avoid water that's too hot or too cold.

Eat a light, healthy meal at least one hour before, allowing time for digestion and to give you energy. Heavy meals, particularly those with lots of carbohydrates, will slow you down, while excessive sugar before a major presentation will overhype you.

Eat slowly to aid correct digestion. Take time to chew your food.

Carry healthy snacks like almonds, muesli bars or fruit so you have energy; your mind needs brain food to aid concentration.

Use Bach flowers or rescue remedy if you are terrified. Speak to a naturopath or your local healthfood shop about 'mimulus remedy' for stage fright.

Have a massage the evening before your major presentation. Massages can release anxiety and tension, and will improve sleep the night before.

Practise some yoga or meditation on the morning prior to your speech or include them in your warm-up routine.

Go to bed early the night before. A good night's sleep will help you to concentrate more effectively during your presentation.

Avoid rushing to your speaking venue or meeting. Take time out to be calm. Time management is the key.

Avoid conflicts or upsets before you see your audience. Clear up any conflict with family, friends or colleagues before you address your audience, or simply be willing to park it to one side and forget it during the presentation.

Find something to smile about. Laughter before a speech will relax you because it releases endorphins. Five minutes smiling or laughing is all it takes. When you laugh, your muscles are activated in the neck, chest, arms, face, shoulders and abdomen. The diaphragm contracts, and residual air in the lungs is expelled. Muscle tension is lower after a good laugh.

15

IMAGE AND GROOMING

It is the costume that transforms actors into characters.
Ngila Dixon, Costume Designer for The Lord of the Rings

Clothing is an important part of your message, so always dress appropriately for your audience. Research says that it only takes seven seconds to make a first impression, and 55 per cent of that depends on how you look.

We put time and energy into what we wear when we attend a wedding, a birthday party or a funeral, because of our respect for the people involved and the occasion. You should treat your clothes for your presentation with the same level of attention.

When planning your outfit for your next presentation, look at yourself in a full-length mirror and ask yourself the following questions:

- How do you want others to perceive you before you say a word?
- What nonverbal message do you want to make?

Then ask someone whose judgement you trust, 'What

words describe me based on how I dress?' If you want to be perceived as professional and authoritative and they respond that you are relaxed and casual, you may want to revisit your outfit. Remember, your speaking image is based on perception, and, like it or not, perception is reality. By avoiding obvious clothing distractions and wearing clothing that suits you and your message, you'll ensure your audience remembers what you said, not what you wore.

A glamorous friend, who was managing director of a public relations company, told me about one of her most embarrassing moments. She was looking after her client, the vice president of an IT company, who, as company spokesman for 44 countries throughout Europe, the Middle East and Africa, was about to make a brand announcement in a television interview. Seconds before the cameras started to roll, she discreetly told him that his flies were undone. My friend then went to the ladies' room, but returned unaware that her own zip was undone! It was left to the embarrassed cameraman to enlighten her.

The story always amuses me, but it contains an important lesson: always keep your clients safe and be attentive to details, but don't forget to double-check your own clothing in the mirror before you appear in public.

Working with a prime minister

In the 1990s, while running my own public-relations consultancy in New Zealand, I was recruited by the then leader of the Labour Party, Helen Clark, as a media adviser. Helen Clark became the country's prime minister in December 1999 but, prior to her win, I spent a lot of time working with her on public image. It's a sad fact that women in positions of power are subjected to more media scrutiny about their clothes and appearance than their male counterparts. There's unequal comment on style rather than substance when it's a woman running for public office. So, in between speech coaching and media consultation, I turned my attentions to her wardrobe. I introduced Helen to several well-known New Zealand fashion designers who could achieve the style Helen was comfortable with – classic, elegant and authoritative.

Helen Clark, unfussed by the latest trends and fashion recognized the role that clothing played in shaping her image and with care and attention in the way she dressed, it was possible to divert the media away from the style and focus on her substance in policy and governance.

Pay attention to detail

Choose your clothes carefully and thoughtfully. Why? Because you will feel calm and in control. Pay attention to every detail, then you can forget about your image and concentrate on what you are saying. Appropriate clothing also helps the audience to listen to your message instead of being focused on your clothing.

I recall coaching a senior manager for an important job interview, using role play and video. We were working through a list of questions when I noticed a bright, loud Mickey Mouse sticking plaster on his finger, which distracted me from listening to his answers. The message was 'I am child-like' rather than 'I am an executive'. The manager explained he'd cut his finger before leaving his house in the morning and had grabbed one of his child's plasters without a second thought. I gave him a clear, neutral plaster to replace it – the full picture matters.

Similarly, dirty shoes or worn-out clothes convey the message that you don't respect yourself. If your audience can see this is how you think of yourself, they won't respect you either. The world treats you as you treat yourself.

Remember to remove all dry-cleaning tags from clothes before you present. I was debriefing a friend after an interview for a managing director's position in London. She looked professional in her black trouser suit – until I noticed, to my horror, a dry-cleaning tag on the inside of her sleeve. We will never know if the interviewing panel noticed, but she got the job!

Dress well and you will send out a signal that you are successful. You will radiate positivity if your appearance is tidy and smart. You will also lift the mood of others and often inspire those you work with also to lift their act.

We all have a disastrous story about not looking good when presenting. Laura's has to be among the most original. She was a director of recruitment, responsible for attracting foreign students to a university, and was due to give a speech to the Health Faculty board. She had rushed from home, having flung on her obligatory corporate suit, but had not noticed that the dry-cleaning hanger was still attached to the garment. She stood to make her presentation – and the board members laughed. Laura said this was the most humiliating moment of her professional career.

A month later, she spoke to the same group. Again in a rush, she arrived breathless and sat down without looking. She therefore did not notice that the chair was broken and it promptly collapsed beneath her. Laura has gone on to make many successful presentations and is known for her passionate delivery, but she thought she was jinxed. In fact, she was merely in too much of a rush and so failed to focus on apparently unimportant details.

Keep it simple

I advise business clients to choose classic corporate clothing for their presentations. After all, you want your personality to shine, rather than being up-staged by your clothes.

Looking the part

Gail, a surgeon about to sit her oral exams for the second time, had lost confidence in her presentation skills. She needed to feel sharp and professional, and her image had to reflect that. At her first exam, she knew her material inside out, but she was so nervous that she mixed up her answers. She needed to find the confidence to communicate her expertise properly. I took Gail shopping for interview clothes, and noticed her posture improving as she changed into an elegant trouser suit. One hour's shopping translated into a boost to her inner confidence. She also cut her hair into a shorter and more confident style.

I'll never forget the elated phone call from her the day she ripped open that envelope and learned she'd passed her exams. Don't be afraid to ask for professional advice if you are stuck or want some new ideas.

Image audit

Consider your wardrobe during the last six months when answering the following questions.

- Are you happy with your current 'look'?
- Have work colleagues commented positively on your appearance?
- Have work colleagues commented on your good presentation skills?
- Did you feel confident networking at the last three social or business functions you attended?
- Do you notice a firm handshake and return it at the same strength?
- Are you confident of your business-dining etiquette?
- Do you have a positive body image?
- Do people compliment you on your interpersonal skills?

- Do you feel you take pride in your appearance (hair, face, posture, clothing, shoes, etc)?
- Does your clothing reflect your personality as well as your company's brand or culture?

If you answered 'yes' to eight or more questions, you have a good level of confidence in your image. Anything less than seven 'yes' answers could suggest that you need to work on your image. If you scored less than four it might be time to call in help!

You can tell me so much about how somebody may perform by their appearance.
Alan Isaac, Former Chairman KPMG NZ

If you are speaking on behalf of your organization, what you wear communicates a message about the company as well as about you. You owe it to your employer to spend some time thinking about the image you project.

I recall talking to a manager about his company's policy on dress code. He was disappointed that some of his staff turned up to work functions in casual clothing when the event fell on a casual Friday. Clients were present at these functions so there were mixed messages about the company's professionalism. While his expectations should have been communicated more clearly to his staff, astute employees could have thought more carefully about appropriate dress or, if they were unsure, asked for clarification. Find out what is expected of you and, if you do decide to dress casually for a function, keep some spare clothing at work, such as a smart jacket, in case you've misread the event.

One business leader turned up to make a speech to a group of young people, or so she thought, but instead was greeted by a business audience wearing black tie. She was dressed in a casual trouser suit, surrounded by people in pearls and furs. She made a wonderful speech but felt she had let down her company's brand.

Take responsibility and double check the details of your presentation. The golden rule is to mirror the audience's dress. If they are formal, dress formally; if casual, dress down. I remember co-leading a four-day seminar in a small town a few years ago. The audience consisted of construction workers and their managers. It was in the hot summer, so we all wore shorts or casual trousers. It would have been inappropriate for me to wear a corporate suit, as I needed them to listen and trust what I had to say.

Style and grooming can be learned

We are not born with style. We learn how to dress. My personal style has developed by observing others who have expertise in this area, usually friends with exceptional flair.

According to a stylist friend of mine Harry Howe, 'Style can be defined by two important things. One is whether a person is comfortable with themselves. So much of a person's confidence is in what they put on, how they treat people and how those people treat them. The second part of style is in taking risks.' Harry also says, 'Be nice to everyone from the cleaner to the CEO – and never wear more than four colours at one time!'

I have always believed in being very careful about my clothing, because I can then forget about it.
Frank Lloyd Wright, architect

Many companies run an induction programme with new employees, setting out their expectations as to dress code. This is excellent practice as the employee then knows what is expected. Most people make an effort on the first interview but dress standards sometimes drop after a few weeks. We need to educate each other about what is acceptable and what is not or provide sensitive and encouraging feedback.

Here are some handy hints when it comes to personal style:

1. Fashion fades, style is eternal.
2. When dressing, be absorbed in yourself; once dressed, be interested only in those around you.
3. Never stop wearing your favourite colour, no matter what shades come out each season.
4. Style is very different from fashion. Once you find something that works, keep it.
5. Dress appropriately for the occasion.
6. Wear your clothes, don't let them wear you.
7. Spend money on two quality items that really work rather than five that don't.
8. Jewellery isn't meant to make you look rich, it's meant to adorn you.
9. The first time a fad comes along in your life, wear it; when it comes back, let it pass.
10. The most important thing is body language – the way you carry yourself, the look in your eyes.

Dressing for success

Robert Pante, in *Dressing to Win*, believes that 'success attracts success'. He states that if you consistently dress as if you were already successful, then you will attract more success. This can be applied to your public-speaking experience – dress as you'd expect a successful public speaker to dress, and you have a better chance of a successful presentation.

A *Management Magazine* article in early 2000, aptly named 'Images made me', quotes a study of top decision makers including CEOs and managing directors. The results: 93 per cent of top executives in the UK and 96 per cent in the US agreed that image makes or breaks your chances of getting ahead.

The sense of being well dressed gives a feeling of inner tranquility.
C F Forbes

Dressing for success was an important part of my life when I ran the Performing Arts School. A large part of my job description was to raise sponsorship and attract money into the business. My audience was the business community. My clothing budget was high, unlike my salary, but the image opened doors so it was money well spent.

Plan your wardrobe

Mary Hooper calls herself an interior designer for your wardrobe. 'Updating your wardrobe is not about being governed by trends. Our lifestyles are constantly changing.'

The reason clothes hang in your closet unworn is because they are not the best clothes for you. It is important to learn what looks best on you, in terms of colour, style and patterns.

Cleaning out your wardrobe and only keeping the clothes you actually wear is liberating and allows you to see whether there are any gaps. I suggest completing a wardrobe inventory of your clothes so you are clear about what clothing you already own and what you still need.

Hair

After focusing on your clothing, don't be let down by unkempt hair. Find yourself a professional hairdresser – ask friends for personal recommendations. I frequently ask my trusted hairdressers to help out when a client is in need of a good cut and style before a television appearance or making a speech. They all concur how presentation is everything – your hair is a part of your body. You can change your shoes and clothes in five minutes but you can't change your hair in that time. Don't skimp on good hairstyling and remember that a healthy diet will also make your hair stronger and shinier. If your hair is looking dull and flat, take a look at your diet because you might be lacking in protein, such as chicken, eggs and fish.

Maintenance

After investing in getting your look just right, how do you make sure you stay looking good right up to the presentation?

Ensure clothes and shoes are ready to be worn before you put them away. Have a sewing kit and attend to loose buttons or hems immediately. Find a good clothes brush – I find the slightly sticky roller type to be the most effective.

Shoes should be regularly reheeled and polished. Look out for the freebie shoe-cleaning kits in hotels. Keep good shoes in a shoe bag and use a shoe tree to help them keep their shape.

Put together a clothes maintenance kit, including a clothes brush, a small sewing kit, shoe polish/shoe cleaner and a small sponge. Have it with you at work or when you travel.

TIPS ON IMAGE AND GROOMING

Wear clothes that make you feel good.

If you are unsure about your style, stick to the classics.

Make sure your clothes fit properly. Be honest about your body, and ask for feedback from people you trust. If store-bought clothes don't fit you properly, have them tailored. Give away or throw out clothing that's too small – don't kid yourself it looks OK if you're really struggling to do up the zip.

Avoid excessive fragrance or cologne, as it can be overpowering. You don't want to knock out the front row of your audience.

Clothing must be spotless, pressed and well tailored. Worn-out and tired clothing makes you look lazy and unprofessional, as if you can't be bothered making an effort.

Wear comfortable, high-quality shoes, and maintain them well. Scruffy, worn-out or dirty shoes distract the audience from your message.

If you're going for the classic look, make sure your shoes are the same colour as, or darker than, the hemline of your trousers or skirt.

Dress lightly, as stress can raise your body temperature.

Long sleeves often project authority and professionalism.

Don't blend in with the wall colour. For instance, if the walls are dark, don't wear a black suit.

Cheap fabrics let you down. Invest in quality garments. Your clothing will last longer, so it's cheaper in the long run.

WOMEN

Avoid heavy make-up – go for the natural look. However, my advice is to wear at least a little make-up if you're comfortable doing so, to avoid looking washed out.

Watch out for panty lines under skirts or trousers.

Provocative clothing is a real no-no – it undermines your credibility. Watch out for G-strings showing above the top of your trousers.

Avoid noisy jewellery – the simpler the better. You want the focus to be on you, not your accessories.

Keep your nails well manicured. Have a regular manicure or set aside time each week to maintain your nails yourself.

Keep a spare pair of tights in your bag in case you get a last-minute ladder.

The higher the stage is, the shorter your skirt will appear. Ideal skirt hems are at mid-knee or slightly below, depending on your work culture.

Consider wearing bright colours. When I give a speech I want you to remember the speaker with red hair and the pink jacket. If you are someone who traditionally wears a black suit, change the routine and buy a brown suit.

MEN
Socks should be the same colour as your trousers.

Always wear a belt. Belts should be the same colour as your shoes.

Wear silk or good-quality fabric ties, and replace them when they're looking worn out. The tip of your tie should finish at your belt buckle.

Make sure the tie pattern isn't distracting to the audience. Cuff links are a more subtle way of expressing your personality.

Watch out for escaping nasal hair, ear hair and chest hair.

If you have facial hair, keep it trimmed and check that it is free of food before presenting.

16

SPECIALIST SPEECHES

My people, my people, listen!
Martin Luther King Jr

For some of us, speaking at a wedding, funeral or office farewell is the most nerve-wracking public-speaking experience of all, because our nervousness is often heightened by the emotions attached to the occasion. We are sometimes more anxious speaking in front of people we know because the outcome matters personally. It can be different when we know we're never going to see an audience again. Many clients ask for help preparing for speaking at family functions. The public-speaking basics discussed throughout the book apply equally to these situations, and this chapter will give you a few extra tips to make this important speech a winner.

Accept invitations to speak

I encourage you to accept invitations to speak at family and social occasions – it's an honour to be asked to contribute to such an occasion and it obviously means a lot to the person asking you, or you wouldn't have been asked. These types of speeches are also a great opportunity to practise your public-speaking skills in front of a sympathetic and supportive audience. Acknowledge that you might be feeling vulnerable, especially at a funeral where you are emotionally involved, and have the courage to speak regardless – you'll be so pleased you did.

Funerals

It is a great honour to be asked to speak at a funeral, whether you are giving the main eulogy or a supporting speech, or would simply like to say a few words about the deceased. Find out what is expected of you – how long will you be speaking for? Have you been asked to talk about the life and achievements of the deceased, or your personal memories of him or her? Ask how many people will be speaking – you won't want to talk for too long if there are five more people speaking after you.

The key to a successful eulogy, as with any speech, is research and preparation. This is one occasion where you don't want to wing it – it's disrespectful and you won't do your best. Write down your speech, and have it with you in case you lose your place. Lastly, if the speech is longer than a minute or two, make sure you rehearse it out loud – you may find that some pieces are difficult to say or don't flow as they should, and the rehearsal will give you the opportunity to rephrase them before the funeral.

If your speech is about the life and achievements of the person, do ask the family if there is anything they'd prefer you didn't mention. A funeral is not the time to settle old scores or score points. Also, be sensitive about using humour – there will be a wide range of people in the audience and an anecdote that raises a smile among a person's friends may be offensive to their grandparents.

Don't feel bad about crying during the delivery of the eulogy – if it happens, it happens. Just be yourself. Worrying about it is just likely to distract you from saying what you want to say. I find it helps to remember that the eulogy isn't about the person delivering the speech – focus on the people who are the main centre of attention and your audience will be with you all the way. Go beyond your ego. You are not here to gain approval or attention, or to please in any way.

I often weave a poem or a quote from Shakespeare into my speech when I read at a funeral. Sometimes you'll find a poem that expresses exactly what you want to say, eloquently and concisely. Sitting up late the night before my dad's funeral I turned to a James K Baxter poem, which said it all for me. I added my own introduction and ending around the poem to form the speech. Reading prose or pre-written text is a great idea if you are upset or terrified of losing control during a speech.

When you are looking for material to include in a eulogy, go with your gut instinct. There are many poetry collections and reference books to quote from, and a search on the internet will also provide many ideas, although they won't all be to your liking. Perhaps there is an author that the deceased person particularly used to enjoy, or a piece of writing that is relevant to their life.

Practical suggestions for writing a eulogy
The following poem was given to me by a funeral director. The author is anonymous. You might find it useful when scripting a eulogy.

When I die
If you need to weep
Cry for your brother

Walking the street beside you
And when you need me
Put your arms around anyone
And give to them what you need to give me

I want to leave you something
Something better than words or sounds

Look for me in the people I have known or loved
And if you cannot give me away
At least let me live in your eyes
And not in your mind

You can love me most by letting hands touch hands
By letting bodies touch bodies
And by letting go of children
That need to be free

Love doesn't die
People do
So when all that's left of me is love
Give me away

For inspiration refer to Charles, Earl of Spencer's eulogy for Princess Diana which transfixed the world when he delivered it on September 6, 1997 in Westminster Abbey. You will find it on the internet.

'Diana was the very essence of compassion, of duty, of style, of beauty,' Earl Spencer said. 'All over the world she was a symbol of selfless humanity. All over the world, a standard bearer for the rights of the truly downtrodden, a very British girl who transcended nationality. Someone with a natural nobility who was classless and who proved in the last year that she needed no royal title to continue to generate her particular brand of magic.'

When he completed the eulogy, which was unashamedly critical of the Royal Family who were seated before him, the mourners in the Abbey applauded. This unprecedented gesture underscores the strength and impact of the eulogy and the emotion it generated.

Another eulogy which moved me was written by a dear friend for her father and described by the presiding priest as the best he'd heard in 30 years as a pastor.

She started with a famous quote from William Shakespeare:

' "All the world's a stage,
And all the men and women, merely players;
They have their exits and their entrances,
And one man in his time plays many parts."

'Certainly not from my pen but that of William Shakespeare's. [she said]

'When I read those words the other day I said to my sister, "Hey Lou, take a listen to this." I read them to her and we both smiled because they captured exactly what we had been thinking about our Dad . . . a man who lived through nearly eight decades and over three continents.

'There were many stages. He played hard. He entered and exited so many scenes in which he played so many parts.'

Note her transition from opening on a classic piece of prose to personalizing and adapting it, in a colloquial style, to describe her dad.

She concluded the ten-minute eulogy with a poem she wrote about her dad's liberation from illness and the immortality of love. This balanced the eulogy beautifully – a finely tuned top and tail which began and ended with poetry.

Simple and heartfelt solutions are a sure way to remember a loved one without pretension and with grace. Children are great at this and should be encouraged to write about the person they have loved and lost.

My young friend Polly, 13 years old, delivered this tribute to her father at his memorial service in Tonbridge, Kent in March 2008.

Mighty Love
There is nothing you can do
Nothing you can say
To bring me comfort in every way
Time will not stop
Life will go on
To me my dad has not really gone
He is there in a flutter
Yet away in a beat
A loving sensation from my ears to my feet
The love is so mighty
My memories so strong
So he shall be with me my whole life long

Weddings

Wedding speeches seem to bring out the best and worst in public speakers – it's such a joyous occasion, and the best wedding speeches hit the right notes of celebration, humour and love that deeply touch the bride and groom and the rest of the audience. But the worst speeches, where the great-uncle drones on for half an hour, or the best man regales the audience with sexist jokes, make you cringe with embarrass-ment. There are a few simple rules to follow if you are asked to give a speech at a wedding to ensure yours is one of the successful ones.

Weddings traditionally used to have three main speakers: the bride's father, the groom and the best man. However, weddings today are often anything but traditional, and it has become usual for the bride and groom to ask a variety of people to speak.

It is very important to ask what material you are expected to cover, and how long you are to speak for. It's unlikely that the bride and groom will expect a thorough retelling of their life stories from birth to the present day. You may be asked to make a toast to a particular person, to provide some informa-tion about the bride or groom, or simply to wish the happy couple well – whatever the expectation, it's crucial that you know it.

The usual public-speaking rules of research, preparation and rehearsal are fundamental to wedding speeches. This is a very important day, so treat the occasion with respect and do your homework.

My former boss, Michael, is a dynamic speaker, and is frequently asked to make a speech at family weddings. His main tip is to do thorough research before the day. 'I ask questions such as what is the style of the wedding, what are your expectations of my speech, what kind of things are important to you? It's important to understand the impact your words will have on the guests attending. Create the appropriate impact for the nature of the occasion and consider the people there. Every wedding is unique – this is the only time that this particular group of people will ever come together. They are nervous so your role is also to break down barriers.'

Inappropriate speeches

Some people seem to think it's appropriate to bring up the worst and most embarrassing moments of the bride or groom's life in their wedding speech. I recall feeling so disappointed after witnessing the 'roasting' of the groom at a wedding – most of the stories seemed to involve drunken escapades that might have been amusing to people in the stories, but certainly weren't funny to the rest of the audience.

Equally embarrassing are stories with obvious sexual undertones – there is no need to get cheap laughs. It adds nothing to such a special event. During one such speech, the unconscious body language of the mother of the bride and the mother of the groom showed their horrified reaction to the best man's speech, which was attempting to entertain and be funny at the expense of the bride and the groom. Don't bring up past partners, racist or sexist comments or stag-night antics, and watch out for your own bias, such as a phobia about marriage.

A wedding is a time when people gather to celebrate and to rejoice, not to mock. It is a privilege to speak at someone's wedding and it's not something that happens very often in your life. You were chosen because you're considered to be a special part of the bride and groom's life. They are relying on your heartfelt speech to create more magic on their day.

Know your audience and rehearse your speech in front of a family member if you are unsure about including sensitive material. If in doubt, leave it out.

Time and effort pay off

Spend time thinking about the special qualities of the bride and/or groom, noting stories that are real, funny, moving and inspiring. Show the human side of that person so that the audience gets to see their unique qualities.

I recall coaching a client who was nervous about speaking at his daughter's wedding. He wanted to get it right so decided to ask for professional advice. We spent two hours mapping out the key messages he wanted to communicate. I suggested he think about a wonderful story describing her as a child and to find a superb baby photo or photo of her doing something exceptional and weave this visual element into the material. He even decided to use PowerPoint at the reception so he could have some photos behind him as he spoke. His confidence grew as we worked on ideas and structure. After the speech, members of the audience congratulated him, saying it was one of the best speeches they had ever heard. Speaking in public was a major challenge for this person, and the successful outcome was due to the effort he put into his preparation.

Putting nervousness into perspective

A Dean of the Anglican Church shared with me a story about a groom overcome by nervousness during his wedding vows:

'One groom was so struck by the immensity of what he was doing that in the middle of his vows, and he was going well, he started to sweat, paled and suddenly fainted straight into my arms! So out came a chair and a glass of water of course, and there in front of everyone we fanned and chatted, and smiled and spoke about this never-to-be-forgotten moment, until he was able to stand up again and with great purpose and determination, he did what he had to and wanted so much to do – made his vow and loved his bride. A great cheer went up and some said afterwards that it was the best wedding they had ever been to!'

If this groom can overcome this degree of nervousness, surely you can overcome yours!

Ideas for wedding speeches

- Aim for a warm tone.
- Find a link between a key event in the year the bride or groom was born and weave it into the opening of your speech.
- Interview family members and friends about their wishes for the couple, and advice for the future – you might find a few gems you can borrow. Take along a dictaphone so you can remember the details.
- Find beautiful baby photographs of the bride and groom. Use them as the props in your speech and present them to the couple at the end.
- What do the couple's names mean? You might be surprised how the meanings fit together.
- What happened on the day in history? There may be a momentous event that happened fifty years ago. Just make sure the event is a happy one!
- Don't include 'in-jokes' – everyone present should be able to understand what you're talking about.
- Keep the jokes and anecdotes relevant and short, and don't laugh at your own jokes.
- Ending on a toast gives you something to work towards and provides a clear ending to your speech.

Tips for a successful wedding speech

- Give a copy of the speech to another guest before the big day and ask him to bring it with him – just in case you lose yours. Don't rely on your memory. Practise the speech on camera to see if it looks stilted and needs reworking. Stay off the alcohol until after your speech – you may not think you're drunk but even a tipsy speaker is embarrassing to watch.
- Make sure you introduce yourself and briefly explain your

relationship to the bride and groom if the MC hasn't done so – otherwise half the audience will wonder who you are.

• Keep it brief – five minutes is probably long enough.

Practical suggestions for wedding speeches

To add a romantic or personal touch when speaking at a wedding, it's worth looking through the passages of poetry and prose from over the centuries. You might find that someone else can capture what you are saying in a few stanzas or, at least, will provide you with ideas and inspiration.

William Shakespeare's love sonnets are a great place to start and one of my all-time wedding favourites is American poet E E Cummings' *I carry your heart with me*.

Other family celebrations

Other occasions where you might be asked to give a speech include twenty-first birthdays, christenings and other milestone birthdays. The rules are the same – prepare well and think carefully about what you want to say. Speeches made on these occasions are remembered for many years, so make it one remembered for all the right reasons!

My brother, Tony, recalls speaking at his daughters' twenty-first birthday celebrations. 'I wanted firstly to honour them as individuals but also in a family and community context. To me their twenty-firsts were celebrations of transitions in life – their journeys from childhood and adolescence to womanhood. I was very conscious of the many friends and other significant people in my daughters' lives who were present to share in their celebration. So I also wanted to use these occasions to perhaps stir in them some of those deep yearnings of the heart that help make sense of life. To achieve this, I drew on memories of childhood, imagery in nature and the concept of dreams. For both my daughters I also incorporated significant music and poetry into my talks to intensify my feelings about this important milestone in their lives.'

I can confirm that the speeches were beautiful and heartfelt, and much appreciated by each daughter.

Thank-you speeches

Thank-you speeches are sometimes planned and sometimes impromptu, depending on the circumstances. If you know it's coming up, prepare and rehearse as for any other speech. If it's a surprise, try to remember the following points:

- Thank everyone as a group, and a few key people individually, rather than listing a large number of people.
- Say why you are thanking the person or audience. Keep it simple and succinct – a gracious thank you and exit is far more compelling than a half-hour ramble.

However, if you have been honoured for something that has taken a lot of work or a lifetime achievement, you may like to outline some of the work you've done, or prepare a speech themed around the goals of the organization you've worked for. It really depends on the circumstances, so think carefully about what type of thank-you speech is appropriate.

Toasts

The dictionary defines a toast as 'a tribute or proposal of health and success, marked by raising glasses and drinking together.' Giving a toast may seem easy, but if you haven't thought it through, it's easy to go blank at the crucial moment. Talk to the people who have asked you to make the toast to see if they have any specific requirements. What do they want your toast to achieve? A toast should only be two to three minutes long, so be sure to time yourself during rehearsal and cut your speech back if necessary.

Deliver the toast standing up, and be aware that you may have your back to some people – if so, consider moving to the front of the room or at least acknowledging the people behind you before starting to speak. When you have finished, raise your glass, say 'To Mum' (or whoever) and take a drink. This action signals the end of the speech.

Farewell speeches at work

When farewelling a work colleague, your goal is to send that person on her way on a high, feeling good about herself. While amusing stories may be funny, make sure they do not mock or humiliate the person – while she may be smiling, off-the-cuff comments can be very hurtful. Mention what you've learned from working with her.

It's great if you can think of a funny prop that you can present as a gift, like a framed photo. I'll never forget the farewell I received from colleagues and board members when I left the Performing Arts School in Auckland that I had founded seven years earlier. The speeches were witty, moving and well thought through. The gift was a stylish gold brooch designed by a well known designer, engraved with a memorable message, which made it all the more special. The speeches left me feeling truly acknowledged for the work I had done, and I cherish the gift because of the thought that went into it.

Welcome speeches at work

If you are introducing new colleagues to the company, make sure you know a little about them – how to pronounce their names, what they'll be doing at the company and a little about their backgrounds.

Your goal during the speech is to put your new colleague at ease. Remember how you felt during your first week at work. Be sincere and make an effort to put thought into your welcome speech.

Master of ceremonies

As a master of ceremonies, your job is to be the link between the different speakers or events. You are the glue that holds the function together, so you'll need to be well briefed about the format, and confident enough to think on your feet if things go off track. The success of your MC experience will depend on how much you know about the function and what is expected of you, so you can prepare properly.

As you are introducing other speakers, you need to know a little about them. Take the time to talk to each speaker before the occasion, if possible, and ask how each one would like to be introduced. Think of yourself as the link between speeches when scripting your own material.

Keep it short – the MC is not the main event. If you talk for too long, the audience will become restless before the main speakers have even started. Keep the mood fun and upbeat.

Ask for an agenda, and stick to it. Your job is to keep the event on track. To do this you should be able to command the attention of an audience. You might like to have a watch on the lectern so you can nod to speakers when you need them to wrap up their presentations. This may not always be appropriate – ask in advance what the organizer would like you to do if speakers take longer than their allotted time.

TIPS ON SPEAKING AT FAMILY EVENTS

Feel honoured – the people asking you to speak have done so because they believe you will add something to the event.

Prepare for a speech at a family event just as thoroughly as you would for a business function.

Your speech should focus on the reason for the event, not on you.

Approach the speech with respect, empathy and love, and you can't go wrong.

If in doubt, ask. Make sure you know what's expected of you.

Be respectful of different cultures, especially if you are presenting to a diverse group of people.

Your speech will be memorable regardless – however, it's up to you how you're remembered.

Use stories and examples to make your points. They will help transform your speech into a glowing performance.

17

SPEAKING CONFIDENTLY TO THE MEDIA

The way to avoid confrontation is pretty simple.
You just answer the question.
Jeremy Paxman, BBC presenter

Many executives, believe it or not, spend many years avoiding interviews with the media because they don't want to be seen to be wrong in public. Their fear is understandable; you put yourself on the line when you appear in public. You open yourself up to criticism. But like it or not, speaking to the media is a vital part of having a senior role and being a spokesperson for your organization. You need to learn how to use the situation to your advantage.

Make it your strategy to work with the media, not against them. Like you, they are committed to doing a good job. It is tempting to blame the media when things get misinterpreted or when you're not happy with what's been written about you; to be honest, I used to do this myself. Eventually I came to understand the two-way relationship business-people have with the media; I needed them to get my message across and grow my business, just as much as they needed a story. I took more responsibility and gave more time to my relationships with editors, journalists and producers. I started to understand how the media really worked.

Don't fear the media

What are we afraid of? We are afraid of looking and feeling stupid, which goes back to the insecurities many of us felt in childhood. We don't want to be laughed at or look or sound unintelligent.

Work at building a rapport with journalists and editors, instead of fighting them. You want exposure to get your messages across. They want to get a good story. They want promotion or career satisfaction, just like you. Circulation and ratings matter to the media, just as profitability matters to the commercial world. We all want the same things in the end. We want to be heard and to be understood.

I always encourage clients to understand the role of the journalist. Most of them are honest and hardworking, just like you. Interviewers new at the job may be more scared than you; try to put yourself in their shoes. Don't judge journalists; rather, understand their motives for talking with you and help them if you can. Reporters are not your enemy, but neither are they 'on your side'; their job is to be impartial and to report the story as they see it.

With a few basic tips and techniques you can be persuasive and confident in the knowledge that you have a story to tell and know how to get your message across with honesty and integrity.

Set the news agenda

All the journalists I speak to tell me that important and potentially ground-breaking speeches often fail to hit the mark because the writer/speechmaker does not deliver the holy grail. What's that? Information that breaks news. When dealing with the media, or trying to ensure that your message is conveyed in print or through the airwaves, you have to play to the editors and sub-editors who decide what will make the news.

I tell my clients that if they want to ensure they run in the evening bulletins, or get a few inches of newsprint, they must deliver a clear, sexy and absolutely new angle or the media will write them off. Say it as it is and make sure it's never been said before.

In December 1992, former Australian prime minister Paul Keating made a key speech to an Aboriginal community in inner Sydney to launch the International Year for the World's Indigenous People. He could have fed the media, and his audience, the usual rhetoric of how Australians, still unreconciled with the treatment of Aboriginal people since European settlement, needed to work harder and pull together and be united. But he had a vision and an agenda – to shift the debate and begin a serious discussion on indigenous reconciliation and the assignment of responsibility.

So he spoke out as no other Australian prime minister has dared to do. 'We smashed the traditional way of life. We brought the disasters. The alcohol. We committed the murders. We took the children from their mothers. It was our ignorance and our prejudice,' he said. It was bold, courageous, shocking, painful. It was also agenda-setting. And the media lapped it up.

During the race for the Democratic Party's nomination in the 2008 American election, Barack Obama, a truly brilliant orator, delivered a landmark speech on race relations which went to the very heart of racism and bigotry in America.

The world's media had gathered at a venue in Philadelphia

on March 18 and cable networks were primed to go live globally with a speech in which the black senator from Illinois had to address the racially divisive remarks of his church's former pastor. It was a make or break moment in the tight race for the nomination against Hillary Clinton.

I believe his speech will go down in the annals of history. Here are some excerpts from it.

Obama on running for president:

> 'I chose to run for the presidency at this moment in history because I believe deeply that we cannot solve the challenges of our time unless we solve them together – unless we perfect our union by understanding that we may have different stories, but we hold common hopes; that we may not look the same and we may not have come from the same place, but we all want to move in the same direction – towards a better future for our children and our grandchildren.
>
> 'This belief comes from my unyielding faith in the decency and generosity of the American people. But it also comes from my own American story.
>
> 'I am the son of a black man from Kenya and a white woman from Kansas. I was raised with the help of a white grandfather who survived a Depression to serve in Patton's Army during World War II and a white grandmother who worked on a bomber assembly line at Fort Leavenworth while he was overseas. I've gone to some of the best schools in America and lived in one of the world's poorest nations. I am married to a black American who

carries within her the blood of slaves and slave-owners – an inheritance we pass on to our two precious daughters. I have brothers, sisters, nieces, nephews, uncles and cousins, of every race and every hue, scattered across three continents, and for as long as I live, I will never forget that in no other country on earth is my story even possible.'

Obama on his former pastor, Reverend Wright:

'I can no more disown him than I can disown the black community. I can no more disown him than I can my white grandmother – a woman who helped raise me, a woman who sacrificed again and again for me, a woman who loves me as much as she loves anything in this world, but a woman who once confessed her fear of black men who passed by her on the street, and who on more than one occasion has uttered racial or ethnic stereotypes that made me cringe.

'These people are a part of me. And they are a part of America, this country that I love.'

Obama on black American disillusionment:

'But for all those who scratched and clawed their way to get a piece of the American Dream, there were many who didn't make it – those who were ultimately defeated, in one way or another, by discrimination. That legacy of defeat was passed on to future generations – those young men and increasingly young women who we see standing on street corners or languishing in our prisons, without hope or prospects for the future.'

Obama on the way to unity:

'This is where we are right now. It's a racial stale-mate we've been stuck in for years. Contrary to the claims of some of my critics, black and white, I have never been so naïve as to believe that we can get beyond our racial divisions in a single election cycle, or with a single candidacy – particularly a candidacy as imperfect as my own.

'But I have asserted a firm conviction – a convic-tion rooted in my faith in God and my faith in the American people – that working together we can move beyond some of our old racial wounds, and that in fact we have no choice if we are to continue on the path of a more perfect union.'

Preparation pays off

Preparation for just about everything in life is the key to success. Being media-trained is the best way of overcoming your fears and is beneficial to anyone in business, politics or any other field that catches the public eye. It is a matter of learning a few techniques to put yourself at ease. Receiving instant feedback from an expert will enable you to come across more naturally next time you are speaking to the media.

Why do you think politicians appear so much more con-fident on television? They are used to it and have the oppor-tunity to practise regularly. For this reason I encourage anyone in business to take regular media-training refreshers so when the real interview turns up you are ready to go. Think of yourself as an athlete; you need to keep your skills sharpened.

My colleague, a former journalist, who is now a top media trainer in Britain recalls the downside of not rehearsing and not being prepared:

'It was back in 1987, shortly after I'd started presenting a regular financial slot on breakfast television. The format of the studio-based slot was to run a couple of brief news items at the start and a US and Australasian market update at the end, leaving room for a live interview of around a minute and a half in the middle.

'In my second week, the producer had arranged for me to interview the CEO of a company that was preparing to undertake one of the prestige engineering projects of the decade. But first he had to persuade the banks to lend him the money, which was why he was keen to appear on my 6.35 a.m. slot with its audience of financial professionals.

'After an innocent enough preamble, my second question to him was: "What makes you so certain that you can complete this project for the sum you have been quoting, when every major infrastructure project in Britain in modern times has gone hopelessly over budget?"

'My interviewee was outraged. He huffed and puffed. He turned red. He proffered a trembling and unconvincing answer and only just managed to contain his rage on air that I should have asked such an impertinent, unhelpful and even unpatriotic question. I put to him a brief follow-up along the same sceptical lines, and with a few more testy words from him the interview was over. Off air, the CEO announced he would never give such an interview again.

'For me, still keen to prove myself, it was a great interview. Not for him though. He had been poorly advised and was perhaps a bit naïve to think that an interview of this kind might be a soft option, a free ad. In commercial broadcasting, you can bet there's no such thing, and public service news programmes won't hold back from asking the difficult questions either.'

The lesson: in this increasingly fast-moving medium you have to have your best shots absolutely at the ready, fire them off rapidly, regardless of the questions, and at the same time be prepared to take the tough questions without complaint. It's rarely personal. It's just business.

Get some perspective

Your first interview is usually the hardest – it does get easier. Dealing with the media can seem overwhelming at times. Yes, it's important, but it's not a matter of life and death. Be clear about your objectives for the interview; as I get older and wiser, I am learning to be less obsessed with how I look and more interested in making a difference to my audience. I am also more concerned to represent my employers and uphold their vision and be true to their brand. When I was younger, the outcome of the interview was very tied up with my ego. Looking and sounding good were all that mattered. Despite my acting experience, I was insecure – this was not about playing a character. I felt there was no costume to hide the real me. Every time these feelings arise, I take a deep breath and remind myself to be real and honest and passionate.

I still make mistakes when speaking to the media; I try to see interviews as opportunities to learn and pass on experiences and stories to potential new clients. Nervousness still creeps in before most interviews, whether they are print, radio or television. It's a natural reaction, but I remind myself that I know how to manage these nerves.

If you choose to be in the public eye you need to learn to toughen up and not take criticism personally. If you are misinterpreted for whatever reason, then let your resentment and frustration go. Learn from your mistakes and resolve not to make them again. If you don't like the way a particular journalist has written about you, you have the power to decide whether you will allow yourself to be interviewed by that journalist in the future. There's no need to burn your bridges, however; remember, you may need that journalist one day.

It can be daunting to read about yourself in the press. On opening night of any theatre production I would fear the presence of theatre critics. I remember a fellow actor, coaching me when I cried about a disastrous newspaper review. 'It's fish-and-chip paper,' she said. 'Don't worry about it'.

Watch the self-criticism

We can be so critical of ourselves. Forgive yourself if you make a mistake. You're not perfect and there may well be an occasion when you cringe with embarrassment because you let your tongue get away with you or you didn't think things through. Move on. Learn from the experience and apologise to your employers or your staff if you need to. But more importantly, apologise to yourself. You are only human.

I am always amazed during training sessions at how self-critical people are about their appearance. Accept the way you look, and accept also that everyone can improve their image through grooming or lifestyle changes. If you can change something, fine, but if you can't, accept yourself as you are. We all come in different shapes and forms. We all inherit different looks and we need to like ourselves more.

Hire quality studios and technology

My media training programmes with clients in the UK take place mostly in a professional studio in the West End of

London with a qualified technician who sets up a real TV studio. This way they can experience the pressure of going through a tough interview with a qualified journalist I have previously arranged, using the latest in broadcast technology. The more real the training, the less scared you will be with an actual live interview.

Before you say yes

Make sure you know the answers to the following questions before agreeing to do an interview.

Who will interview you?

If your interview is with a radio or TV programme, find out whether it will be a taped or live programme, and who will be conducting the interview. Which news organization do they work for? If you are invited to a dinner party with a friend, you always find out the name of the hosts and some background about them. You may choose to decline the interview if you're not comfortable with the personality of the interviewer.

What are their contact details?

Who do you call if you need to check or change arrangements before the interview? If a reporter rings you to arrange an interview, make sure you get contact details so you can get in touch with her should you need to. Always promptly return phone calls.

What do they want to speak about?

Find out what general issues will be discussed. Why do they want to do this interview? Who is the audience? This may influence the type of questions you will be asked.

Why do they want to speak with you?

Why you? This isn't a rude question; it means you can properly prepare for the interview. Are you the best person to speak on this subject?

When do they want to speak to you? For how long? Where?

Journalists work under the constant pressure of deadlines, but this doesn't mean you have to answer questions right away. Be polite and, if necessary, say you cannot comment immediately. Promise to call back at an agreed time and keep your word. Being rude to a journalist is a good way to ensure a negative write-up for you and your message.

Once you've ascertained you're the best person to do the interview, and agreed the terms on which it will take place, it's time to prepare your material, your appearance and your frame of mind to ensure you perform well.

What to do in an interview
What's your SOCO?

Have a clear and accurate understanding of your message. Work out your SOCO – the single over-riding communication objective. What is the core issue that you want the journalist to remember?

If you are associated with an organization and its brand, you become an ambassador during interviews. You have to be very clear about your key messages – rehearse them and ensure they are consistent with your organization's brand.

We teach clients in media training to speak in sound bites. A sound bite is a short, succinct phrase, about 15–20 seconds long, which has a clear message you want to get across. Practise summarizing your key messages aloud.

However, don't try to rote learn your answers; you need to

be able to talk naturally about your topic, not recite your answer regardless of the question. I recall a conversation with a producer of a television news show, who joked, 'I don't want you polishing your clients up too much.' I laughed and told him we were simply helping people to feel more relaxed and ready for questions, which in turn helped the interviewers to do their job. Too much rehearsing is dangerous because a lack of spontaneity harms your credibility.

Anticipate the tough questions and prepare for them
What are the five most difficult questions you might be asked? Practise your answers. Role play with a colleague until you are comfortable with your response. Think about whether a difficult question can give you the opportunity to lead into making your key point.

The eyes have it
Always maintain eye contact with the journalist. Eyes darting at the floor or ceiling can make you look shifty or nervous; you want the viewers to think you are polite and trustworthy. If you look like you are avoiding eye contact, your audience won't trust you.

Don't panic if the interviewer is not looking at you. Keep on looking at the interviewer. You'll be able to read the interviewer's body language if you focus on him. Never look down the camera lens when giving your answers. Eye contact means you more readily establish rapport with someone.

I notice in my training sessions that this is often one of the most difficult behaviours to change. In real life we don't always maintain eye contact. We talk and reflect on our thoughts and often have our eyes elsewhere. So when practising this, it can seem false. Don't worry. With practice, you will find that looking people in the eye becomes natural, even powerful. Try focusing on just one eye. It's not a staring-down session, so if the other person becomes uncomfortable, look away momentarily. Study her body language. If this makes you lose attention and miss what she's saying, focus on her mouth and her words. Then when it's your turn to speak, return to her eyes so they can see you speak with integrity.

Be aware of your body language

Sit up straight. Pull your shoulders back. Stand tall and you will breathe correctly and appear confident. Avoid hunching up. Your diaphragm needs to be able to do its job. It is designed to enable your breathing by pushing out your stomach and allowing your lungs to fill. Bad posture will lead to shallow breathing, less oxygen flowing to the brain, and your responses will slow.

Look confident and be yourself. Spontaneous gestures make you look expressive but there is nothing worse then gesturing for the sake of it. Only gesture naturally. Some people have been told they are over-dramatic with their gestures and they need to sit on their hands. I don't believe you can gesture too much. As long as it looks and feels natural, just do it.

If you feel self-conscious about gesturing while you speak, try freeing your hands by not clasping them, or holding the arms of the chair. This will allow you to tap into your natural gesticulating ability. Once you start moving your hands, you will be amazed how well you'll capture your audience's attention and convey your meaning.

Voice

Project your natural voice. Diction is particularly important on television and radio. Enunciate the vowel sounds clearly. Pause naturally and be careful not to speak too fast. Pay attention to pace. Refer to Chapter 4 for more information about using your voice effectively.

Clothing

How do you want to be perceived? Avoid stripes and spots on television as they can strobe. Wear a jacket if you are being interviewed for a business audience. Classic clothes are best unless you are a fashion designer and this is a part of your message. The two main problem areas are women wearing short skirts and low-cut tops, and men wearing ties that clash with their shirts. Refer to Chapter 15 on image and grooming for more information.

Do a warm-up

Stay calm, focus, be relaxed, turn your mobile phone off and have faith in yourself. You are an expert in your field. Tell yourself this. Use positive self-talk and affirmations as discussed in Chapter 11. Warm up your voice if you are in a quiet place and practise some breathing exercises. This is particularly important before a television interview. Stretch, move around to get your blood pumping and centre yourself by quietly warming or limbering up your body. Anything you do to relax your mind is good. Laughing releases endorphins which will make you feel confident. Yawning opens the back of the throat, which also relaxes the jaw; humming exercises the vocal cords.

Do what is best for you. You know what relaxes and energizes you more then anyone. I often go for a walk a couple of hours before an important interview to run through my messages and to feel energized, then shower and freshen up. I like to be alone for a few hours before an interview to get away from all distractions and chatter.

On television

Think about the main points you want to get across. Make sure you get these messages out; you don't necessarily have to wait for a question to be asked. Many politicians are very skilled at getting their points across and not directly answering the question. Watch the news regularly and observe this technique.

Pause and breathe. Take your time. You don't have to rush or answer straightaway. Take at least two or three seconds to collect your thoughts.

Be prepared for an invasion of your personal space – the interviewer may need to sit very close, or a camera may be put in your face. This is necessary to achieve the framed shots; don't let yourself be unsettled.

If you're caught on the hop

Sometimes, journalists may ring you for a comment without pre-arranging an interview. Remember, you don't have to talk to them! In fact, if you're not comfortable with your topic, it isn't advisable to start answering questions immediately. Give yourself time to consider the request – journalists will usually agree if you say that their call has been unexpected and you will ring them back when you've had a little time to think. If you do agree to speak to them, you should ask:

- Are they taking notes of what you're saying?
- Are they recording what you're saying?
- Are you live on air (in the case of radio)?

If you don't want to speak with journalists, say so at once. Otherwise, journalists will assume that you have no objection to being interviewed or quoted.

Be aware always that in this new millennium, technology now enables faster and more intrusive coverage and often deprives the person in the media spotlight of adequate time to prepare and indeed time away from the public gaze. One wrong word, one gaffe or one slip-up and internet sites like Youtube and Myspace will be broadcasting it around the world instantaneously. Broadcast networks and traditional press scour such sites for possible stories, so if something goes wrong, or you have a cross word or altercation in public, which then finds its way onto the internet, it could potentially end up in traditional broadcast outlets. Be alert and be aware! Someone with a small digital camera could be lurking just around the corner! Thanks (or maybe not) to the internet everybody these days thinks of themselves as a news-gatherer.

Media photographs

If your interview is with the print media, you may have the opportunity to provide a photograph for the newspaper or magazine to include beside the article. Experienced photographer Monty Adams suggests the following when choosing a photographer:

- Use a professional photographer; ask around to find out who's recommended.
- Always have a good selection of clothes for the photo shoot, or consider hiring a stylist. If you don't have appropriate clothes, borrow or hire them.
- Women can hire a professional make-up artist to make them look fantastic.
- Being organized is essential – give yourself lots of time so you don't have to rush during the shoot.

Common pitfalls

No comment

Never say 'no comment' in response to a question. You'll look as if you have something to hide. Think of something less evasive to say, such as 'I can't answer that question because the information is confidential,' or 'I don't have that information right now, let me get back to you.'

Off the record

With journalists, nothing is ever 'off the record'. Don't put yourself in a vulnerable position by sharing information you don't want the journalist to print; whatever you say can end up in quotes in any media. I confided in a journalist once 'off the record' and it ended up in a national newspaper the next week. I was furious, but the damage was done.

A good journalist will refuse to allow you to tell them anything on the basis that it can't be published, which is what most people understand by the term 'off the record'. Very simply, it's not in their interest to listen and it places them in a compromising position if they hear the same information from another source. However, some very astute media commentators will feed or 'leak' information to a journalist, on the basis that it is not *attributed* to them. This is entirely different from 'off the record', and is a high-risk strategy regardless of how well you think you know the journalist. In the end, most journalists are willing to sacrifice a good contact for the sake of a good story, so I recommend saying nothing that you would object to seeing in print or hearing on air with your name attached.

Watch your tongue

'We can make this really complicated or we can make it very simple.' This is the advice of Julie Walters, a former journalist with the *West Australian* newspaper and now managing director of Media Speak, a successful UK media training and communications company which she set up in 2000 with her husband, Peter Coe. Her mantra reflects my own: say it as it is.

Keep your answers brief; say what you want to say, then wait for the next question. Journalists often pause a moment before asking their next question; sometimes interviewees feel uncomfortable with silence and rush to fill the gap with more information than they originally intended to provide. Say what you intend to say and then stop talking.

Be aware of what you say when the interview is 'officially' over. Journalists get some of their best stories in the toilets or in the elevator on the way out.

Jargon
Say it simply. Be aware that the journalist may not be a technical expert in your field, and even if he is, the publication's readers almost certainly won't be. Don't assume they have the same level of understanding of the subject matter as you.

Listen carefully to the question
Don't let the reporter put words in your mouth. If your answer is summarized incorrectly, be clear and correct any misstatement.

Be prepared to say 'I don't know'
It is OK to tell journalists you don't know the answer to their questions. Always try to suggest someone who might be able to help, or undertake to find out and get back to them with the answer after the interview.

It goes without saying that you should never lie in an interview. Even a little white lie has the ability to land you in hot water; and one small exaggeration or twist on the truth and you instantly lose credibility for everything you say. Likewise, never pass on hearsay or rumour. If you are asked about something that concerns someone else, refer the reporter to that person for comment.

Can I read the story before it goes to print?
Journalists pride themselves on being fair and impartial. Asking if you can preview a story before it goes to print implies that you don't trust them. Don't embarrass yourself by asking; the journalist will refuse and you'll have antagonized him just as he's preparing to write the article.

The one exception is if the subject matter is technical; you could then offer to review the technical content of his work to ensure there have been no misunderstandings. Extracting a promise to review before it goes to print is often easier with a technical or professional publication than with a newspaper, radio station or TV channel. They will be less defensive about a perceived 'approval' process denting their objectivity. On the other hand, this is not a public-relations exercise. You might get one chance to look at it and suggest changes. But in the end it's their story and they will have the final say.

What do the journalists advise?
Focus on the interview at hand
Richard, a journalist friend, recalled one of his best interviews – it was with the deputy prime minister of Israel.

'He didn't muck around; he went straight to the point and was extremely focused. He wasn't looking around for the next person to talk to.'

Richard's advice to all those being interviewed 'is to be honest and true'. He says you need to commit to what you're saying and own it. Richard has two wonderful facial expressions, which say 'talk to me' and 'beckon and engage'.

Listening is a skill in itself. The professional listener will extract information with a nod, a smile, or a quizzical look, and in so doing lead the interview subjects to say more than they originally intended.

Remember to relax and smile. Peter Coe from Media Speak has a story with some valuable lessons. One of Britain's leading providers of media and presentation skills training, Peter spent more than 15 years presenting news programmes from London for the BBC and before that for the hugely popular breakfast television channel, TV-am. He tells a revealing story about his own first faltering steps as a presenter on its flagship daily programme, 'Good Morning Britain'.

'I was just 25 when I arrived at TV-am as a young journalist with almost no experience in television. But the company itself was young and awash with opportunity for those who shared even some of the ambition and energy of Bruce Gyngell, the station's Australian MD.

'So it was that after a couple of years as a news producer on the overnight desk I was encouraged to audition, successfully, for the vacant role of presenter for the breakfast show's new finance spot. Frankly, it was a role I was seriously under-qualified for. Not only had I never presented live before, even on home video let alone broadcast television, but neither did I know much about finance. And the only training I ever received was a one-hour studio rehearsal the day before my screen debut.

'Here I was: expected to broadcast between 6 and 7 a.m. five days a week, to look bright-eyed and cheerful and sound as if I knew what I was talking about. Worse still, the director wanted me to give the camera and the nation a million kilowatt smile as the programme's opening titles faded to reveal the show's main presenters – and me – sitting cosily round the breakfast table in the studio's fake kitchen.

'For two whole weeks, that's ten shows, my nervousness and discomfort were embarrassingly evident. I could not manage a smile. My face was numb. Thankfully, I was sitting down because most of my body felt rigid too.

'Every day for those first two weeks and for some time after, I pored over that morning's tape to see how bad I'd been. But the wonderful part of it was that, fuelled by my desire not to return to the overnight desk, I gradually became more and more relaxed. Little by little, I even enjoyed going live; to be myself in an artificial and yet exposed environment. I smiled!

'There were at least three lessons I eventually drew from this uncomfortable baptism:

'Firstly, the experience I went through was so like the trauma faced by people learning to give corporate presentations when, like me, they're not born performers.

'Secondly, to get better at presenting you have to work through the pain. You have to put up with feeling and looking awkward the first few times you're out there, with the sense of failure when you know you haven't performed well and, sometimes, with the criticism or even indifference of others. The crucial thing is to acquire the flying hours and gain confidence simply from doing it and then doing it again a little bit better each time.

'And thirdly, unlike my experience, you can gain a huge amount from preparation, in the form of thoroughly knowing what it is you're going to talk about, rehearsing your performance, ideally filming and playing it back, and getting plenty of constructive criticism from people whose judgement and frankness you can rely on.'

Don't let the technology faze you

Even the experts don't always get the technology right all the time. Do not be fazed by technical hiccups – a dictaphone that jams, a camera that won't record, PowerPoint slides that won't come up on screen. 'Something always goes wrong with technology so just relax.'

Jim Mora, television presenter and friend, recalls an interview with Bob Geldof where the tape recorder wouldn't work. 'Bob was affability itself, helping us to sort out the technical problems. Sometimes when we want things to go well, we are thrown when they don't. If you are overly "keyed up" then you don't welcome the unexpected, but the unexpected can often break the ice advantageously.'

Don't act as if you're best friends with the interviewer

I asked a senior journalist advice for people being interviewed by media. 'I think there are two little things that people need to remember when being interviewed on radio or TV. Firstly, don't use the host's name all the time. Once at the beginning and once at the end of the conversation is enough. It sounds false if you keep using their name all through, and overfriendly.'

She went on to say, 'The other thing to remember if you are on air and the host greets you, is that there is no need to ask how they are. For example, if the announcer says, "We're talking today to Jane Smith, a marine biologist from NIWA . . . Good morning, Jane," Jane should simply say "Good morning" and wait for the first question. Asking "How are you?" is superfluous and prevents the interviewer from getting on with the interview.'

TIPS ON SUCCESSFUL MEDIA INTERVIEWS

Set the news agenda. Be bold, new and fresh. Grab the headlines.

Be enthusiastic. If you're not excited about your subject matter, no one else will be.

Prepare some 'sparklers' – interesting anecdotes about your subject material – which you may get the opportunity to use during the interview. Paint pictures by telling stories, so your audience can understand you more easily.

Identify the angle – what's the real story here?

Pay attention to what you wear – ask yourself how you want to be perceived.

Body language matters. Journalists and viewers will pick up on subtle signals, so ensure your facial expressions and gestures are consistent with your message.

Speak clearly, especially during radio interviews, as the audience cannot see you.

Get to the point – an interview is not the time to waffle.

18

EVALUATING YOUR PRESENTATION

Tell me the truth – I can take it!

Being evaluated by others is never easy. The only way we can improve is to allow others with more experience to review our performance. Put your ego aside – how do you think top presenters became so good at public speaking? Other speakers, teachers and mentors helped them to refine their skills.

Ask for feedback after every time you speak in public. When I pitch for new business I always ask a colleague to have a 'debrief' with me after the presentation. How did I do in that meeting? Did I listen enough? Did I take too long to get to the point? Did I go off on a tangent? Feedback on these points helps me to improve my presentation next time around.

Asking for feedback or planting a friend in the audience to comment on my performance is the best way I know to improve my presentation skills.

Put your ego away

Constructive criticism of your presentation is not criticism of you as a person. Have the confidence and self-belief not to take feedback as a personal attack, but simply as a way of improving your presentation skills. One of the authors who has influenced me in this area is psychiatrist Dr Gerald Jampolsky, formerly of the University of California Medical Centre in San Francisco. As he aptly says in his book *Love Is Letting Go Of Fear*, 'To experience unconditional love, we must get rid of the evaluator part of ourselves. In place of the evaluator, we need to hear our strong inner voice saying to ourselves and others, I totally love and accept you as you are.'

During one of my 'Train the Trainer' workshops, I recall a consultant who refused to be evaluated. He was a great presenter, but was afraid of his presentation skills being criticized. Accepting constructive feedback hasn't always been easy for me either – it's tempting to feel I've failed miserably if a presentation hasn't received a glowing evaluation. When I suggest to clients that they might be feeling insecure about feedback, some laugh and say they're fine, but years later they sometimes admit they weren't able to distinguish between feedback on their performance and criticism of them as a person. Self-acceptance comes with many years of practice.

Feedback is an important part of the learning process. Even if the feedback is offered in a clumsy manner, focus on the learning point instead of taking things personally. And remember, you don't have to agree with every comment – it's only someone's opinion.

Get it in writing

Evaluation forms are excellent because you can refer to them later and refresh your memory about key learning points. If you are receiving verbal feedback, take some notes rather than relying on your memory.

If you are appearing on radio or television get someone to tape it and debrief the outcome with someone you respect. You can usually buy a copy of the interview from the television station. I also do this with print interviews, as it's the only way I learn how I can do better next time. It's not obsessive – rather, it's professional and shows that you care about the quality of the work you do.

Watch and read the audience

The audience's reactions are the best indicator of your presentation's success. They will let you know with their body language, with their comments and with their applause. Stay around afterwards to find out what they think. You will know by the number of people who come up to you. I get some of my best feedback when I allow time to speak to people afterwards. Don't be afraid to ask, what did you learn? I love it when I receive an email from a stranger telling me what they took away from my speech, or see someone taking notes during a presentation.

If you're in the audience and have been particularly impressed with a presentation, please take the time to let the presenter know, either in person or in writing. I promise they will really appreciate it, regardless of how experienced they are at public speaking. After attending an entertaining and inspiring speech by Glenda Jackson, I sent her a copy of my written feedback on her presentation, simply because I know how important it is to speakers to know how their audience reacted. She phoned immediately to thank me and commented on how much she appreciated it. We all need feedback.

Two minds are better than one

Before your presentation, always share your speech with someone for critiquing, paying particular attention to the beginning and ending. Likewise, ask someone to cast an eye over any written material you intend to distribute during the presentation – spelling and grammar mistakes make you look sloppy. You may even get some new ideas or anecdotes that you can work into your speech.

Guidelines for giving feedback

Giving feedback is a huge responsibility – you can easily devastate a person's confidence with throwaway comments. You have a responsibility to ensure that your comments are well thought through and empowering. Ask yourself – if I was receiving this feedback, how would I like to receive it?

Focus on the positive first

Praise is essential when people have done well. People need to hear what they've done well, as well as what they can improve on. Follow the Commend – Recommend – Commend sequence of feedback. For example:

'Your energy is motivating and I love your enthusiasm for your subject.' [Commend]

'However I feel distracted when you play with your wedding ring while you are speaking and look down at your notes for long periods. I want you to relax your hands and leave your ring alone and connect more with us by lifting your head and making eye contact.' [Recommend]

'Your speech is so well written and conversational I am absolutely riveted to every word.' [Commend]

Be constructive

By making feedback constructive you will be helping the person to find out what needs to be done rather than just telling them what they are not doing right. Always look for areas of improvement rather than concentrating on what went wrong. However, giving only positive feedback allows no room for improvement, so make sure you do offer some constructive criticism as well.

Emphasize what you see and hear

Make your feedback descriptive rather than evaluative. Describe your own observations without making judgements as to whether you see the facts as good or bad, and leave people to make up their own assessment. 'Did you know you said "um" ten times during your introduction?' is better than 'You sounded nervous and ill-prepared.' Reward behaviour you want to reinforce with a positive comment.

Be specific

Make feedback specific rather than general. It is easier for someone to react to this than to general statements. Be straightforward and use objective, not emotional, words. Instead of a broad comment such as 'Your speech was too technical,' be clear about what part of the speech you're refer-ring to, such as 'When you talked about car maintenance, you assumed that your audience knew the different parts of the engine.'

Be realistic

Direct your comments towards actions that the presenter can control. Make your feedback practical and realistic, including specific suggestions for how the presentation can be improved. Take into account the experience of the person to whom you're giving feedback – the type of feedback you give an experienced presenter will be different from that for someone who has just given his first public address.

Encourage self-criticism

People are more willing to accept criticism when they recognize their own strengths and weaknesses. Start by encouraging them to appraise themselves and then build on their own insights. I like to ask clients to review their own performance after seeing it on film.

Don't rush it

Take time to explain things to the person properly. Rushed feedback with no opportunity for discussion leaves room for misunderstandings.

Be timely

Feedback should be immediate – if you wait a week to debrief you won't remember the presentation in enough detail to be specific. Set up a structured time to give and receive feedback.

But nothing

Watch out for 'but' when giving positive feedback. Saying, 'You were great, but . . .' is a mixed message and can be confusing.

Pick your points

If you overwhelm people with too many suggestions, they are likely to feel frustrated. Focus on the points that need the most improvement.

Focus on them, not you

Feedback is about helping the person receiving the feedback, not demonstrating your superior knowledge. Also, be aware that you can only offer your opinion, and the person receiving the feedback doesn't have to agree with you. Using 'I' statements, such as 'I became confused when you jumped between topics' helps the person to realize that you are offering your opinion, and that other people in the audience may feel differently.

When there's a group

If you're debriefing with a team of people, appoint someone to lead the feedback session. This ensures that everyone gets the chance to share their opinion with the group.

Implementing the advice

Receiving feedback can be frustrating if there isn't an opportunity to practise the suggestions in the near future. Try to set up another speaking engagement so you can put the pointers into practice. Also, if giving feedback, check that the person has understood what you're saying by asking them to tell you what points they have learned from the feedback session.

Watch for body language

You can often tell how the person is responding to the feedback through their body language. If you sense they are feeling vulnerable or unhappy, limit the feedback to one or two points and focus on building their confidence.

Keep an eye on your own body language as well – if your words are in conflict with your tone or facial expression, the person receiving the feedback will believe your body language rather than the words you say.

Evaluation Sheet

Develop your own evaluation sheet based on this suggested outline.

RATING:

5 *Excellent:* very happy with the presentation
4 *Very good:* quite rewarding to listen to
3 *Competent:* some good points, some not so good
2 *Needs work:* somewhat disappointing to listen to
1 *Very disappointing:* take the opportunity to improve and upskill

CATEGORY	RATINGS	COMMENTS
Opening Was the opening stimulating and powerful? Did it capture the audience's attention? Did it have impact?	1 2 3 4 5	
Manner Direct, confident, authentic, calm, professional, lively, bold, powerful, gentle, caring?	1 2 3 4 5	
Content Was there a logical beginning, middle and end? Did the speaker use stories, anecdotes or metaphors to illustrate points?	1 2 3 4 5	
Body language Natural, relaxed gestures, good posture? Confident, expressive?	1 2 3 4 5	

CATEGORY	RATINGS	COMMENTS
Facial expression Smiling, expressive, open, no twitching?	1 2 3 4 5	
Eye contact Alive, energetic, looking at the audience?	1 2 3 4 5	
Vocal quality Varied pitch, pauses, good pace, passionate?	1 2 3 4 5	
Volume Easy to hear? Projection?	1 2 3 4 5	
Language Is it appropriate for the audience? Jargon?	1 2 3 4 5	
Group participation Did the audience get involved? Any questions?	1 2 3 4 5	
Tone Energetic and enthusiastic? Passionate or boring?	1 2 3 4 5	
Ending Powerful, memorable, challenging, finishes with a bang?	1 2 3 4 5	

Strengths – Three things I did well

1. _____

2. _____

3. _____

Opportunities – Three things I could improve on

1. _____

2. _____

3. _____

Other comments

1. _____

2. _____

3. _____

BIBLIOGRAPHY AND RECOMMENDED READING

A brilliant easy read is *Building Confidence for Dummies*, written by British authors and business consultant, Brinley Platts and Kate Burton. Other useful books are:

Adler, Stella, *The technique of acting* (New York, 1990).

Barkworth, Peter, *About acting* (London, 1991).

Bell, Chip and Zemke, Ron, *Managing knock your socks off service* (New York, 1992).

Braysich, Joseph, *Body Language* (New York, 1979).

Brown Glaser, Connie and Steinberg Smalley, Barbara, *More power to you* (London, 1992).

Buzan, Tony, *Make the most of your mind* (New York, 1988).

Cairnes, Margot, *Approaching the corporate heart* (Sydney, 1998).

Chapman, Elwood, *Your attitude is showing* (London, 1992).

Chopra, Deepak, *Ageless body, timeless mind* (Sydney, 1993).

Colbin, Annemarie, *Food and healing* (New York, 1996).

Decker, Bert, *The art of communicating* (California, 1988).

Desikachar, *The heart of yoga* (Vermont, 1995).

Eswaran, Vijay, *In the sphere of silence* (Singapore, 2005).

Evans, Eileen, *It's a great life when you're well* (Auckland, 2000).

Farhi, Donna, *The breathing book* (Sydney, 1996).

Fisher, Helge, Knox, Jacqueline, Robinson, Lynne and Thomson, Gordon, *The official body control pilates manual* (London, 2000).

Gawain, Shakti, *Creative visualization* (California, 1978).

Gelb, Michael, *Present yourself* (California, 1988).

Greene, Bob and Winfrey, Oprah, *Make the connection* (New York, 1995).

Godefroy, Christian and Barrat, Stephanie, *Confident public speaking* (London, 1999).

Henderson, Robyn, *How to master networking* (Sydney, 1997).

His Holiness the Dalai Lama, *The little book of wisdom* (London, 1998).

Howard, Ken, *Act natural* (New York, 2003).

Jampolsky, Gerald, *Love is letting go of fear* (California, 1979).

Lamerton, Jacey, *Everything you need to know – public speaking* (Glasgow, 2001).

Leigh, Andrew and Maynard, Michael, *Perfect presentation* (London, 2003).

Linklater, Kristen, *Freeing the natural voice* (New York, 1976).

Maltz, Maxwell, *Psycho-cybernetics* (New York, 1987).

Maysonave, Sherry, *Casual power* (Texas, 1999).

Peoples, David, *Presentation plus* (New York, 1992).

Pante, Robert, *Dressing to win* (New York, 1984).

Pease, Allan and Barbara, *The definitive book of body language* (London, 2004).

Ratcliffe, Gail, *Take control of your life* (Sydney, 1995).

Rodenburg, Patsy, *The right to speak* (London, 1993).

Stanislavski, Constantin, *An actor's handbook* (New York, 1963).

Stuttard, Marie, *The power of speech* (Auckland, 1994)

Tourles, Stephanie, *365 ways to energise body and mind* (Vermont, 2000).

Walters, Lilly, *Secrets of superstar speakers* (New York, 2000).

Whiticker, Alan J., *Speeches that shaped the modern world* (Sydney, 2005).

INDEX

Also in the Right Way series

GOING SELF-EMPLOYED

How to Start Out in Business on Your Own – and Succeed!

Steve Gibson reveals why some new businesses take off and others flop. He shows how to assess whether you've got the right characteristics to set out on your own and how to avoid pitfalls that trap the unprepared.

As a self-employed business start-up trainer and adviser, Steve Gibson has helped hundreds of new ventures to succeed. In this book he shares his knowledge in a clear, encouraging style, adding practical tips from those already running their own thriving businesses.

Find out how to:

- Produce a workable business plan

- Research your market thoroughly

- Achieve excellent sales

- Handle tax, national insurance and VAT

- Target your customers and keep them happy

- Promote your business

Make sure your entry into the world of self-employment is a success!

To order these Right Way titles please fill in the form below

No. of copies	Title	Price	Total
	Internet Marketing	£7.99	
	Successful Property Letting	£9.99	
	Going Self Employed	£5.99	
	For P&P add £2.50 for the first book, £1 for each additional book		
	Grand Total		£

Name: _____

Address:_____

_____ Postcode: _____

Daytime Tel. No./Email _____
(in case of query)

Three ways to pay:
1. Telephone the TBS order line on 01206 255 800.
   Order lines are open Monday – Friday, 8:30am–5:30pm.
2. I enclose a cheque made payable to **TBS Ltd** for £_____
3. Please charge my ☐ Visa ☐ Mastercard ☐ Amex
   ☐ Maestro (issue no. _____)

Card number:_____

Expiry date: _____ Last three digits on back of card:_____

Signature: _____
<small>(your signature is essential when paying by credit or debit card)</small>

**Please return forms to Cash Sales/Direct Mail Dept.,
The Book Service, Colchester Road, Frating Green,
Colchester CO7 7DW.**

Enquiries to readers@constablerobinson.com.

Constable and Robinson Ltd (directly or via its agents)
may mail, email or phone you about promotions or products.

☐ Tick box if you do not want these from us ☐ or our subsidiaries.

**www.right-way.co.uk
www.constablerobinson.com**